THE ART OF HEALING YOUR WOUNDED INNER CHILD

AN EMPOWERING CBT SKILLS & EMDR THERAPY WORKBOOK

with Journal Prompts to Overcome Childhood Trauma, Build Self Compassion, Effectively Set Boundaries, and Find Peace

NORA GRACE

Table of Contents

CHAPTER 4: RECONNECTING WITH AND REPARENTING THE CHILD INSIDE.................29

CHAPTER 5: EMBRACING FORGIVENESS, NURTURING COMPASSION, AND FINDING RELEASE
....47

Your Inner Child Bonuses

https://zenmonkeybooks.com/inner-child-bonuses

Embarking on the path of inner child healing is a transformative journey, where the resilient spirit within meets the tender echoes of the past. These bonuses will provide a valuable foundation for starting your own personal healing journey. Each one is designed to guide you in motivating ways, offering guided meditations, reflective prompts, a daily mood tracking journal, and uplifting affirmation cards that all nurture self-compassion and encourage deeper exploration of your own childhood experiences.

By engaging with these bonuses, you'll gain clarity on identifying emotional triggers, build resilience through mindful guided meditations, and cultivate the strength to embrace your authentic self with renewed understanding. Ultimately, these tools aim to empower you to take the first courageous steps toward emotional freedom and inner peace.

BONUS 1 Guided Personal Growth Meditations to promote self-healing and wellness. There are five nurturing 10-minute guided meditations that are designed to focus your thoughts on self-care, relaxation, and mindfulness.

BONUS 2 Shadow Work Journaling Guide and Letters to Your Inner Child Workbook, both focusing on fostering a caring relationship between you and your inner child. These two powerful tools were created to get you on the fast track to your personal healing journey.

BONUS 3 Daily Mood Tracking Journal crafted to cultivate self-awareness, a key component to the personal healing journey. This daily journal will accompany you on your personal healing journey. You will have an opportunity to assess and reflect on the interactions of your day and how they may have impacted your mood, mindset, and emotional wellness.

BONUS 4 Self-compassion Affirmation Card deck designed to build self-esteem and resilience. Your self-compassion practices start with developing care for yourself. These little reminders are a great way to start your daily routine. Focusing on one reminder per week can promote feelings of happiness that will carry you through the good and challenging days ahead.

Are you ready to begin your amazing personal healing journey?

Let's get started!

HOW TO USE THIS WORKBOOK

Welcome to a journey of profound self-discovery and healing. This workbook is designed as a companion to guide you through the process of reconnecting with and healing your wounded inner child. As you embark on this path, it's important to understand how to effectively utilize this resource to foster genuine change and emotional healing. Positioned strategically after the table of contents and before the introduction, this section aims to prepare you for the transformative experiences that lie ahead.

Getting Started

Before you dive into the exercises and reflections, take a moment to ground yourself in your intentions. Why have you picked up this workbook? Perhaps you've carried the weight of unresolved childhood trauma, or maybe you feel stuck in patterns that no longer serve your well-being. This workbook is crafted to address these deep-seated issues by guiding you gently toward healing the scars left by past experiences.

Structured for Healing

The workbook is divided into themed sections, each focusing on different aspects of the inner child. You will encounter exercises designed to unearth and confront the unresolved emotions from your past that continue to influence your life today. Through guided reflections, journal prompts, and practical activities, you'll learn to recognize and soothe the parts of yourself that are still hurting.

How to Engage with This Workbook

- **Create a Dedicated Space:** Healing requires space and privacy. Designate a quiet, comfortable spot to work through the exercises without interruption. This physical space can mirror the mental space you'll need to explore your inner landscape.

- **Schedule Regular Time:** Healing doesn't happen overnight. Just as physical wounds need time to heal, emotional wounds do too. Set aside regular time in your schedule to engage with your workbook. Whether it's a few minutes each day or a more extended session once a week, consistency is key.

- **Reflect and Write Freely:** Use the journal sections to express your thoughts and feelings freely. Don't worry about grammar or style; focus instead on honesty and depth. Writing can unearth emotions and memories buried deep, allowing you to process them in a safe environment.

- **Move at Your Own Pace:** Some sections may resonate more deeply with you than others. It's okay to spend more time where it feels necessary. If a particular exercise brings up intense emotions, take a break if needed. This journey doesn't have to be rushed.

- **Use the Tools Provided:** Each chapter includes specific tools and exercises designed to tackle different aspects of healing your inner child. These might include visualization exercises to reimagine your childhood experiences or affirmation practices to rebuild your self-esteem. Use these tools to craft a healing regimen that suits your personal needs.

- **Revisit as Needed:** Your healing journey might require revisiting specific exercises or sections. As you grow and heal, new insights might emerge, making it beneficial to return to earlier exercises with a fresh perspective.

Embrace the Journey

As you work through this workbook, remember that healing is not a linear process. Some days will feel more challenging than others, and old wounds may resurface. This experience is a normal part of the healing process. Each step you take is a step toward understanding yourself better, fostering forgiveness (both for yourself and others), and building a healthier, happier future.

By engaging with this workbook, you're taking a courageous step towards healing the wounds of your past. Allow yourself to feel, understand, and gradually let go of the pain that has held you back. Now is your time to heal, grow, and discover the joyous life you deserve. Embrace this journey with an open heart and mind, and watch as you transform.

Welcome to Your Journey of Transformation

This workbook empowers, inspires, and guides you toward personal growth and fulfillment. Take a moment to commit to yourself and this journey by reading and embracing these intentions:

Commit to Being Honest: I will approach this workbook honestly, confronting my thoughts, feelings, and behaviors openly and truthfully.

Commit to Consistency: I will consistently engage with this workbook, recognizing that steady, deliberate effort will lead to meaningful growth.

Commit to Self-Compassion: I will treat myself with kindness and patience, understanding that progress is a journey and setbacks are part of the process.

Commit to Growth: I will step out of my comfort zone, embrace new perspectives, and challenge myself to develop new skills and habits.

Commit to Transformation: I will allow myself to change and evolve, celebrating each achievement and using obstacles as opportunities for learning.

Your Name: _____ Date: _____

By writing your name and the date above, you're making a promise to yourself. This page represents your readiness to invest in your well-being, unlocking your potential one step at a time. Let's begin this journey with purpose and passion!

INTRODUCTION

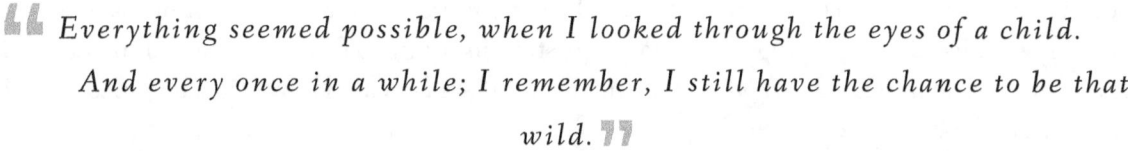

> *Everything seemed possible, when I looked through the eyes of a child. And every once in a while; I remember, I still have the chance to be that wild.*
>
> —Nikki Rowe

No matter how old you've gotten, you still have yet to grow. There is a deep, hollow feeling within you, one you're still trying to make sense of today. That is what has brought you here. The memories that play across your mind remind you of the hardship you faced when you were young. You've tried to move on from the pain, but it lingers, looming over you like a dark cloud waiting to burst with rain.

These memories have consumed your life. This pain is one you've known for as long as you can remember. You've been forced to live with the fear that you won't ever leave the suffering behind, that it will be a part of you forever. I'm here to tell you that it won't. I know what it's like to feel the physical turmoil, the pressure overtaking your body, and the anxiety that snowballs into an unimaginable force.

I was once paralyzed by anxiety, depression, and self-doubt. I sunk deeper into those negative feelings, desperate to claw out. Sometimes I wondered whether I'd ever know true happiness and contentment again. I felt so powerless, so overwhelmed that I had no idea what to do. I put off facing the difficult memories of my childhood because I was aware of how hard it would be to revisit them.

I became an empty shell, someone who went through life mechanically, barely surviving by the skin of her teeth. I finally arrived at a point where I knew there was no going back. Either I took the time to heal, or I'd drown in my pain until it swallowed me whole. I chose to heal. I decided to give myself the chance to rediscover the light in my life, to focus on the good, and to work through the bad.

You're about to embark on a journey that will completely and wholly transform your life. By the end of this workbook, you'll have a better relationship with yourself, and you'll finally be free. You'll be free of the burden that is your pain. You'll be able to enjoy life again and look toward the future with excitement in your eyes. You won't be afraid to live your life any longer. This workbook is your chance to truly heal.

I wouldn't be where I am today without the help of EMDR therapy. EMDR stands for "eye movement desensitization and reprocessing." It is a form of psychotherapy used to treat individuals who have experienced trauma (Corcoran, 2024).

I encourage you to use this workbook while working with a therapist to support you through the EMDR steps. A trained professional can assess when you're ready to move on to each step of EMDR. Remember, this approach will take time.

You'll need to work slowly and carefully to comb through the events of your childhood and process the memories you encounter. A trusted therapist will help to create a safe space for more challenging inner child work as you move through EMDR therapy.

"I don't know if I can do this. I don't know if I'm ready." I've said these words to myself countless times during my journey. Like any positive change, I struggled to stay consistent in trying to heal. I fell back into old, familiar bad habits. The anxiety and depression didn't go away in an instant when I decided it was time to remedy my situation. It took time, effort, and patience.

I want to remind you that you're on no one else's timeline but your own. Think of this workbook as a path to guide you toward becoming the person you've always wanted to be. Think of it as a roadmap filled with adventures, some more difficult than others, but each with a lesson. You will face moments where you want to quit, where the memories uncovered may be too much to deal with.

During those moments, remember how you felt when you were in the thick of it. Picture how uncomfortable and uneasy you were, so much so that you sought out this book in the first place. Leaving your healing journey halfway may seem easy at first because you don't have to brave the pain, but it's still there. No matter how much you try to mask it, the pain will always stick around until you do something about it. Are you ready to meet your inner child? They've been waiting a while.

Chapter One

A FRIEND WITHIN

> *You try all your life to be an adult, but something deep down inside you will always be that child.*
>
> —Viv Albertine

It all seemed so simple back then. The days felt longer, the emotions coursing through you stronger, making everything you did feel like an adventure. When you think of your childhood, you focus on the good, the little moments of true joy, because to think of anything else brings you too much discomfort. You might be thinking, "My childhood wasn't all bad. There were good times. Maybe I'm overthinking things. Maybe there's something else wrong with me that has nothing to do with this."

We've all felt this way. We've all tried to shut our feelings out and force ourselves to believe that our childhoods were filled with purely good times when they most likely weren't. There is a reason you feel the way you do. There's a reason that you struggle with your emotions, have difficulty trusting people, and worry you'll never be good enough.

Imagine that little boy or girl inside of you, the one whose face you've seen in old photo albums, the one with a smile so innocent you wonder how that ever could've been you. You may not have thought about them in a long time. They're still there, showing up ever so often to remind you that there's work to do.

You deserve to be happy and feel free the way you dared to when you were little. I know what it's like to leave that creative, happy little child behind, convinced that it was time to grow up. I had no idea how differently I'd see her now that I have. I look back on the times I struggled, wishing I could take that little girl into my arms, squeeze her tight, and tell her everything would be okay.

I wanted her to know that she was finally understood, that everything she had to say was finally heard. Don't ignore your inner child. Let them out. Let them roam free so you can learn more about them. You won't be able to move on from the darkness you carry now until you face where it came from. It all starts with a bit of reflection.

Rediscovering Your Childlike Wonder

What is wonderment? Wonderment is when you feel amazement, awe, and excitement about the simplest things. When you were a child, that feeling came naturally to you. You'd spend every day exploring and learning all the new things life had to offer. You never had to question it. It was a part of your everyday experience (Willey, n.d.). What were some of the things you liked doing as a child? Maybe you liked to climb trees in your backyard until the sun went down or to dig for treasure in the soil between the flowerbeds. I used to like to spend my afternoons out in the front yard, setting up picnics for my stuffed animals and collecting flowers to make perfume. I never thought about what was happening around me, how much time had elapsed, or where I needed to be once my mom told me it was time to head inside.

I was thoroughly captivated by that activity without a worry in the world. While we may not have that luxury as adults, we do have the ability to rediscover all of the wonderful things that made life worth living. Your first thought may be, "I don't have time for anything else. Every day, I'm fighting to keep my head above water." I was right where you are. My daily schedule was so packed that I couldn't conceptualize the idea of adding more to it, even for a little delight.

I realized I didn't need to set aside hours to find my wonder. I didn't have to sacrifice the time I spent on work or my family to enjoy myself. All it took was a shift in mindset that allowed me to appreciate the little things. Here are a few steps you can follow to bring wonder back into your life:

- **Find a little joy every day:** If you're anything like me, from the moment you get up to the moment you go to bed, the only thing on your mind is your to-do list. It's constantly changing, depending on the day, but it fills you with immense stress. You worry about the house becoming a mess, ensuring your kids are fed and happy, and taking care of work for the day. There are happy moments, but you never really stop to enjoy them because you're always trying to get ahead. Finding joy in your day-to-day life doesn't mean creating a new routine. It means to appreciate what you have. It means to relish how incredible your coffee tastes in the morning, how it feels crawling into bed after a hot shower, reading a book you love, or watching a television show that helps you relax. There is so much to love about what we experience, but we sometimes get too caught up in doing rather than living.
- **Spend some time outdoors:** Think about all the time you spent outdoors as a kid. You climbed trees, rode your bike down the street, played in the sprinklers, and dug around in the back-

yard. The warmth of the sun on your face lulled you, and the cool afternoon breeze made you feel calm. Getting outdoors as an adult who's constantly moving from one task to the next can feel impossible. However, spending even a few minutes outside can give you the reset you're looking for. Step out with your morning coffee. Take the kids out to play. Get your work done on your laptop on the back porch. It took me a while to see that a little sunlight was the answer to a lot of my problems. So, get some fresh air, go for a walk, and soak up all that nature has to offer.

- **Reflect on the details:** When was the last time you really looked at the things around you? How long has it been since you stopped to notice how much the tree in your backyard has grown? The world around you is changing every day, even when you feel stuck, even when the days start to meld together. Your senses are a lot more powerful than you realize. The things you see, hear, smell, and touch all influence you in some way. You can find genuine inspiration in the simplest of things if you really look. So, the next time you're out and about, take in all of the details the way you would if you were a child. I see the way my two children look at the world. They have such wonder, such excitement in their eyes even when we're just at the grocery store. Bask in the beauty of your surroundings, note how they make you feel and remain present. You're going to look back on this time and think, "Things were actually really good then. I wish I could go back." Make the most of what's happening right now.

- **Step away from your phone:** We're all guilty of scrolling a little too much. The hours pass us by, and we don't even realize it. You tell yourself that you'll scroll for a few minutes to get out of your head, but what ends up happening is that you waste too much time, or you feel worse when you're finished. When you were a kid, the last thing you were worried about was keeping up with other people. You didn't need endless amounts of information at your fingertips every second of every day. You knew how to be present, to fully engage with what you were doing, and it's time you find that again. Put your phone away for an allotted amount of time every day. Separate yourself from the noise so you can focus on what's important. I started by acknowledging how many times I picked mine up to scroll. Then, I started timing how long I spent on social media, which made me incredibly uneasy. Acknowledging where my time went helped me cut back and now, I'm able to utilize the hours in my day much more wisely. Take note of where your time is going, how it's being spent, and how it makes you feel overall.

- **Slow down and take it all in:** Your world feels like it's moving too fast. The endless unfinished to-do lists weigh heavily on your mind. You're tired of every day feeling the same, and you long for that refreshed, rejuvenated feeling. The way to make that feeling yours is to slow down. Your worth is not determined by how many things you can get done in a given time frame. You don't have to exhaust yourself to succeed. What you need to do is prioritize your mental and physical health, even if your day is incredibly busy. All you need is a handful of minutes to collect yourself, clear your head, and give yourself what you need to keep going. During those few minutes, nothing else exists. Work doesn't exist, responsibilities don't exist. All that exists is you and what makes you feel good. Integrating these moments into each day will slowly change your life. It will change how you feel and keep you from burning out.

Healing Exercises

Finding your wonder starts with understanding the things that fulfill you. With this exercise, you're going to choose one activity that you can commit to doing once a week. That could be starting a passion project, baking some treats, or going out for a meal.

Next, you'll choose one small activity you can do in a few minutes that you can do every day. That could be journaling for five to ten minutes about what you're grateful for, reading, meditating, stretching, or just relaxing.

Here is what your two activities could look like:

- Going out for a Meal: once a week.
- Reading: two pages every day.

I love to spend my Sundays going out for a meal with my family or friends. It helps me take my mind off my responsibilities, share a few good laughs, and enjoy delicious food. There are weeks that I think about skipping it altogether, telling myself that I need to stay home and take care of the things I'd been putting off, but I don't. That time is meant to help me decompress, to let go of the worry for a little while. Not only is it helping me to relax, but it also gives me something to look forward to when the week gets a bit crazy.

My daily habit that I consider self-care is reading. I set a goal to read at least two pages of my book before I sleep, and even though I usually end up reading more, it's an easy goal to achieve. Reading serves as an escape from stress, but it also allows my creativity to run wild. I feel so inspired while reading, and it makes it so much easier to slow down.

Choose your activities and make them a part of your daily and weekly routine. They will cause quite a significant, positive change in your life, but it will also open your mind up to reconnecting with your inner child.

Looking through the Eyes of a Child

Have you ever stopped to think about what life is like through the eyes of a child? If you have trouble uncovering your childhood memories, try looking to other children for guidance. You could have a few younger cousins, siblings, nieces, or nephews who can help you with this. Children can teach you so much about life if you pay attention. You'll be a lot more likely to live in the moment and find joy in the little things when you see things from their point of view (Raypole, 2020).

Raypole notes, in his article published in *Healthline*, that you can reconnect with your inner child by engaging in creative play with children (Raypole, 2020). Think of the time you've spent with a child in your family. It could've been that you were roped into playing Legos with your little cousin at his birthday party for an hour. Perhaps you attended a tea party with your little sister, helping her set up her stuffed animals in their assigned seats.

Any creative play can help shake loose those memories from your childhood. It can remind you of simpler times and help you see the good, and even the bad. I experienced a moment when I played with my nephew, watching him set up his toy cars for a race. I watched his mother finish up what she was doing and rush over to play with him. She didn't mind that her phone was ringing off the hook and buzzing with new notifications from work. She was present with her baby boy.

Seeing that unleashed an emotional ache within me. It reminded me that I didn't have that kind of relationship with my mother. My mother would always put herself before everyone else. She expected all of her children to fall in line, despite her inability to parent us. While I cannot say everything she ever did was bad, there was certainly a lack of emotional support in our relationship. Her actions made me recognize just how emotionally detached I became as an adult. I was terrified to trust people. I was scared to open up for the fear of being judged.

Over time, I learned a lot from my children and the other children in my family. I saw how much of a difference I could make in their lives. I knew how to approach each challenge due to the trauma I dealt with when I was their age.

Looking back on old times and revisiting your childhood memories can be heartwarming and painful. You can experience both emotions at the same time. Think about how you would feel if your childhood self sat right in front of you. What would you do? What would you say to them?

Healing Exercise

For this exercise, I want you to pull out a piece of paper and a pen. You'll start by addressing the letter to your childhood self. I want you to write out everything you wish you could've told them. Write to them like they're sitting before you, waiting for someone to tell them that everything is going to be okay.

Writing this letter is your first step in healing the wounds that have traveled with you to adulthood. Don't be afraid to let all of your thoughts out during this exercise. Don't hide anything. Don't be ashamed of the way you feel. I know that there is a lot you wish you could fix about your past, but remember, these were things that happened to you. The trauma you experienced during that time was not your fault.

You were just a child. You were supposed to have people around you who loved you unconditionally and heard you when you told them you were hurting. It's time you confront all of the darkness you've been carrying and have a genuine, honest conversation with the person you once were.

Heartfelt Reflection: A Journey Within

Embarking on this journey of self-discovery, you are invited to delve into the depths of your emotions and experiences. The Heartfelt Reflections section serves as your personal canvas, where you can express, explore, and examine the intricate details of your feelings and memories. It's a space dedicated to your inner narrative, allowing you to articulate and confront your vulnerabilities and strengths.

Guided Reflection: Facing Self-Doubt

Consider a moment when doubt crept in, whispering that you were not enough. Reflect on this experience:

Identify the Moment: When did this feeling last overwhelm you? Pinpoint the situation that sparked this self-doubt.

_____

_____

_____

_____

Detail Your Experience: Describe the circumstances that led to these feelings. What were the triggers? Who was involved? What exactly happened that made you doubt yourself?

_____

_____

_____

_____

_____

Explore Your Emotions: Dive deep into how you felt during this moment. Was it fear, sadness, frustration, or a mix of emotions? Write them down openly and honestly.

_____

_____

_____

_____

Reflect on the Impact: How did this episode affect your behavior and decisions? Did it change how you view yourself or your capabilities?

_____

_____

_____

_____

Continued Healing and Growth

Your journey thus far has been marked by a significant shift toward nurturing your inner child—offering them the love, compassion, and attention perhaps long denied. This healing path began the moment you chose to prioritize your well-being and explore new avenues for growth, stepping away from the stagnation of old pains and fears.

Moving Forward without Rush

As you proceed, it's vital to remember that healing is not bound by deadlines or expectations. Progress at your own pace, invest sincere effort and embrace the gradual unveiling of your inner self. Allow your inner child the freedom to emerge and shine, reflecting the growth and understanding you've gained. Now marks the start of your journey, unique and unbounded by time—cherish and nurture it.

Throughout your life, you've been trying to understand why you feel the way you do. You wonder why you can be a little too sensitive sometimes, why you shut down when things get tough, and how much effort it takes to return to normalcy. I didn't know how much of an effect my past had on my present until I began searching through the memories for the truth. It wasn't just about the hardships I faced. It was about the fact that I learned how to cope with trauma and process my emotions as a child.

When we were little, we were learning every day. We'd watch our parents, mimic their behaviors and apply them to our lives, and sometimes, this wasn't a good thing. Healing your inner child means acknowledging the wounds, discovering what caused them, and moving forward.

There will be times when you feel stuck and you wonder if this will all be worth it. During those moments, you remind yourself why you're doing this. Remember, every effort you make matters. Every single time you get back up to help yourself makes a difference. You're only at the beginning of your journey. Are you ready to continue?

Chapter Two

WHAT IS EMDR?

" *The past affects the present even without our being aware of it.* **"**
—Francine Shapiro

A memory leaps to the forefront of your mind, and you're instantly transported back to your youth. It's like you could feel the warmth of your mother's hug on your skin, smell the scent of her perfume before she left for work, and for a moment, you think that maybe you got it all wrong. You try to convince yourself that the difficult memories you have were just fabrications put there to help you make sense of the pain.

You try to connect the sweet, fuzzy memories with the difficult ones and wonder which side of the story is true. Both sides can be true at the same time, and that was something I learned quite early on in my own inner child work journey. I realized that the good memories didn't negate the bad ones, and while there was a lot about my childhood I enjoyed, I still had wounds for a reason.

The person you are today is a direct reflection of your childhood. All of the behaviors you possess were learned when you were young. While some may have changed over time, the foundation of your life was created when you were too small to understand. Whether you have a clear picture of your childhood trauma or you're still trying to uncover it, you can still benefit greatly from Eye Movement Desensitization Reprocessing (EMDR) therapy.

What Is EMDR and How Can It Help Me?

According to Dr. Katherine Compitus's article published in *Positive Psychology*, EMDR therapy is a type of exposure therapy used to treat PTSD (post-traumatic stress disorder) and other phobias. (Compitus, 2020).

This process was created by Francine Shapiro in the eighties when she noticed "certain repetitive eye movements paired with distressing thoughts, would reduce the intensity of those thoughts." (Compitus, 2020). While observing her own behavior as she concentrated on her distressing thoughts, she saw that her eyes would dart back and forth. She came to the conclusion that when a person faces trauma, it causes them to feel so overwhelmed that their regular coping mechanisms may not work (Compitus, 2020).

This trauma causes the brain to label the distressing thoughts and memories as sensory rather than factual. The internal wounds are why you feel negative sensations when those memories resurface before you truly focus on the recollection itself (Compitus, 2020). When we're processing trauma, trying to focus on the logical side of things can be quite a challenge. Our emotions get in the way, making it difficult for us to work through the pain.

EMDR therapy helps to remove the emotions associated with those distressing thoughts and memories. That way, you'll be able to recall those memories without all of the negative feelings overwhelming you (Compitus, 2020). Your body wants to heal itself. It wants to be rid of the trauma, to feel better, but due to the way your painful memories are currently stored, it's like you're reliving them all over again.

Healing Exercises

This exercise will follow a self-administered form of EMDR therapy. It's essential to note that while engaging in this exercise, you might feel emotions that impact you negatively. Self-administered EMDR therapy should not be used to treat severe trauma, phobias, or PTSD. A trained therapist should address these matters.

However, if you're dealing with minor stressors, anxiety, or moderate depression, this form of EMDR therapy can certainly help you.

This exercise follows integrating bilateral stimulation into your routine to help you cope with difficult memories. Bilateral stimulation stimulates the body and brain in a rhythmic right-left pattern (Rowell, n.d.). It creates balance, which allows you to separate the emotions you feel from the memories themselves. Again, it's important to note that this should not be used to handle unbearable trauma.

I want you to step outside for a short ten-minute walk. For the first minute, let your mind run wild. Allow your thoughts to swim freely around in your mind, and when that minute is over, envision them disappearing. Shift your concentration to putting one foot in front of the other, grounding your mind. Take the time to search inward to process your emotions while you focus on the movements themselves.

The Eight Phases of EMDR

EMDR therapy is traditionally done in an eight-phase treatment model. The duration of treatment and the amount of sessions needed for each phase can vary. This process is different for everyone. Your therapist will work with you to determine how long this process will take. This treatment should be conducted by a trained professional. Discovering more about EMDR can help you understand the many benefits it has to offer and whether it's a viable treatment option for you.

EMDR therapy played an integral role in my ability to heal my wounded inner child. Without it, I wouldn't be where I am today. If you're looking to engage in EMDR therapy but don't have a trained professional to help you, I suggest you find someone well-versed in this process. With the knowledge of the technique itself at your disposal, you'll be sure to get the help you need. Here's a look at the eight phases of EMDR:

Phase One: Introductory

At this stage, your therapist will work with you to understand your history while planning the appropriate treatment. Your therapist will help you to draw out the most distressing memory first to use as a target. This could be an early childhood memory or trauma you experienced during that period. EMDR follows a sequential form of processing so when you start with the right target, you'll also address other stressors.

Phase Two: Client Preparation

During this phase, you and your therapist decide where you want to go and what you want to do first. Together, you will discover what success looks like for you. Remember, EMDR is a form of trauma therapy, and engaging with painful emotions can be both difficult and harmful if not handled properly. You will form a therapeutic alliance with your therapist, establish rapport, and be given more information on the method. During the process, your therapist will teach you valuable techniques to use if a session has to be redirected when processing a difficult memory or event.

Phase Three: Assessment

In this phase, you and your therapist decide which memory to target first. Your therapist will guide you through a discussion of your past, helping you to lure out the memories you may have suppressed. You will be looking for the root cause of your trauma, the reason behind all of the pain that has followed you throughout your life. Your therapist will ask you to identify the most distressing image of that trauma, something you can associate with that time. An example could be a photograph that captures the environment, sensations, and emotions that are tied to that specific memory. You will need something that transports you back to that period, so you can better understand the event overall.

During this phase, your therapist will ask you to explain the negative beliefs about the target event. You may say things like, "I deserve to feel miserable." You will be asked to rate your distress level on the SUD (Subjective Units of Disturbance) scale where 0 indicates "no disturbance" and 10 represents the "worst disturbance." (Brooks, n.d.). Your therapist will ask you to think about the positive belief you'd want to feel instead, such as "I deserve to be happy." They will be measured using the VOC (Validity of Cognition) scale of 1-7. If you select 1, it means you think your positive belief is false. If you select 7, it means you think your positive belief is true. (Brooks, n.d). These scales will help you to identify what you think of your positive and negative beliefs, which will determine the next steps of your treatment.

Phase Four: Desensitization

You will be asked to meld the distressing memory with therapist-guided bilateral stimulation. This change will remove the negative emotions associated with that distressing memory so you can focus solely on the facts. You'll be able to recall that memory without feeling overwhelmed by your emotions. Your therapist will ensure that you maintain a clear sense of self-efficacy, or a sense of control, throughout this phase. Challenging your beliefs can feel like an uphill battle, but with the right safety protocols, you will make it through. During desensitization, you might feel uneasy when you first bring up the memory. To combat this, you can visually "bring in" someone or something, such as a wise person, spiritual animal, or another avatar, to soothe you while you navigate that memory (Compitus, 2020).

Phase Five: Installation

Your therapist will utilize the VOC scale to help you replace your negative self-beliefs with positive ones. This stage is critical, as it completely rewrites what you've probably thought about yourself for a very long time.

Phase Six: Body Scan

You'll be asked to recall the original distressing memory to see if it's still considered sensory. If you still have negative emotions and sensations attached to that memory, it's clear to your therapist that you haven't fully processed that memory yet. Your therapist will work with you to determine whether you need more time to process that particular memory or if there's another one that needs to be addressed first.

Phase Seven: Closure

Here, you will apply the self-control techniques you learned in earlier sessions. Your therapist will help you review them and ensure they're adequately integrated. The purpose of this stage is to help you find balance. You will have learned different self-soothing techniques that will aid you in dealing with any new stressors that may surface. You'll be asked to keep a record of any new disturbances, such as dreams, uncomfortable body sensations, thoughts, or other feelings you'd need to address in further sessions.

Phase Eight: Re-evaluation

You'll review your progress with your therapist, along with which aspects have worked, and which haven't. You'll be able to determine whether you need to continue treatment on the current memory or change the target entirely. Remember, if you reach a point where you feel like you haven't gotten enough out of EMDR therapy, don't be afraid to try again. It might not work as effectively the first time, but it does open your mind up to the possibility of confronting your pain and healing. You haven't failed EMDR therapy if there's still work to be done. You're simply aware of what your next step is and that's to continue (Compitus, 2020).

Heartfelt Reflections: A Journey Within

Journaling can be a profoundly effective tool in your healing journey, especially when combined with therapeutic approaches like EMDR and inner child healing. Here are some thought-provoking journal prompts designed to complement these therapies by encouraging deep introspection and emotional expression:

Identifying Moments of Impact: Think back to a vivid, early childhood memory. Describe the scene as if you are there again. What do you see, hear, and feel? After you've set the scene, reflect on how this moment might still be influencing your life today. What emotions arise when you think about this memory now?

_____

_____

_____

_____

_____

_____

_____

_____

Dialogue with Your Inner Child: Write a letter to your younger self at an age when you felt vulnerable. What words of comfort or support do you wish you could have heard back then? How can you offer that same comfort to yourself today?

_____

_____

_____

_____

_____

_____

_____

_____

_____

_____

_____

Before and After EMDR: Reflect on a recent EMDR session. Describe your emotional state before and after the session. What changes did you notice in your thoughts, feelings, and physical sensations? What specific memory did you work on, and how do you feel about that memory now?

_____

_____

_____

_____

_____

_____

_____

_____

Healing Visualization: Close your eyes and visualize a safe place where you can meet your inner child. Describe this place in your journal. What does it look like? How does it feel to be there? Imagine a conversation with your inner child in this safe space. What would you talk about? What does your inner child need from you?

_____

_____

_____

_____

_____

_____

_____

_____

_____

_____

_____

Patterns of Behavior: Identify a pattern of behavior you wish to change. Can you trace this back to your childhood experiences? Write about the origins of this behavior and how it served you in the past. Now, reflect on how it affects you in the present. What new behaviors would better serve you today?

_____

_____

_____

_____

_____

_____

_____

_____

Forgiveness Pathway: Forgiveness can be a powerful aspect of healing. Is there anyone, including yourself, that you feel ready to forgive? Write about what forgiveness means to you in the context of your healing journey. How might forgiving this person (or yourself) impact your healing process?

_____

_____

_____

_____

_____

_____

_____

_____

_____

_____

Celebrating Growth: Reflect on the progress you've made in your healing journey. What are some significant changes you've noticed in yourself since beginning EMDR and inner child therapy? Celebrate these victories, big and small, and write about how each step forward has made you feel.

_____

_____

_____

_____

_____

_____

_____

_____

_____

Future Hopes: Look to the future and write about what you hope to achieve through continued healing. What aspects of your life do you think will improve? How do you envision your relationship with yourself changing?

_____

_____

_____

_____

_____

_____

_____

_____

_____

_____

_____

_____
_____
_____
_____
_____
_____
_____
_____
_____
_____
_____
_____
_____
_____

These prompts are designed to help you delve deeper into your subconscious, confront past traumas, and nurture a compassionate relationship with your inner child. By regularly engaging with these reflections, you can enhance the therapeutic work of EMDR and inner child healing, fostering greater self-awareness and emotional resilience.

Your inner child may have some pent up emotions that you have pushed back for years. It can be hard to explore them, and even more daunting to confront them. The upcoming chapter will guide you through the ins and outs of the emotions of your inner child.

Chapter Three

THE EMOTIONS OF YOUR INNER CHILD

> *The most sophisticated people I know - inside they are all children.*
>
> —Jim Henson

Welcome to a pivotal chapter in our journey of self-discovery and healing. In this section, we delve deep into the heart of our emotional landscape to confront and address the suppressed emotions of our inner child. For many of us, our earliest years were not just times of joy and discovery but also of pain, confusion, and neglect—emotions that, without proper attention, have lingered silently within us, shaping our adult lives in ways we might not fully realize.

Understanding and confronting these suppressed emotions is not merely about revisiting past traumas but about acknowledging and validating the feelings we experienced, no matter how difficult. This process is crucial because our unresolved emotions can manifest as fears, insecurities, and destructive behaviors that undermine our happiness and relationships.

This chapter, we will explore practical strategies and exercises designed to safely bring these hidden emotions to the surface. We will learn how to listen empathetically to our inner child, offer comfort, and ultimately integrate these feelings into our conscious self. By doing so, we not only free ourselves from the shadows of the past but also open the door to a more authentic, joyful present. Join me in this courageous step toward emotional clarity and liberation.

Confronting the Emotions of a Wounded Inner Child

The emotions you feel every day dictate your actions and reactions. When you feel good, you're more likely to be productive, content, and fulfilled. However, when you're anxious, stressed, frustrated, or angry, you feel like the entire world is against you. You grow bitter about every little thing, and your sense of gratitude dissipates.

What emotions do you feel most daily? When I first answered this question, I wanted to say that I was happy most of the time, and I didn't let my anxiety win, but that wasn't true. I was in my head more than I wanted to admit. I felt physically drained every day, going to bed at night only to wake up just as exhausted the next morning. I suffered from debilitating panic attacks that got in the way of my daily activities. I fought off the nausea and fatigue that came with those attacks, trying to maintain a normal life, but it felt impossible.

Eventually, I began distancing myself from everything and everyone I cared about. I wanted to be alone because I believed I could protect myself that way. I wouldn't have to push myself out of my comfort zone. I wouldn't have to feel anything that made me uncomfortable or scared. I wanted nothing more than to exist without the pain, but I started to long for a happy life again. Shutting myself away wasn't the answer, and I knew that, but for so long, I was afraid of doing anything about it.

I was afraid to brave the idea that I needed help. Not only would I need to seek out a professional, but I had to do some inner healing work if I ever wanted to be better. For years, I rocked back and forth between wanting to try again and wanting to quit. What changed for me was the realization that I would eventually grow old with those negative feelings looming over me. I didn't want them to take over my entire life. I didn't want them to keep me from being happy.

I took the leap by finding a therapist and beginning my EMDR therapy, which certainly helped, but I did also learn quite a lot on my own. I forced myself to get excited about the journey, removing any expectations I had by concentrating solely on progress.

A whirlwind of emotions will sweep you off of your feet when you reopen old wounds. That is why you need to know how to navigate your feelings, rebuild the foundation that has had its cracks in it for a while, and learn to live a happy, fulfilled life. That all starts with acknowledging that no matter how hard things get, something can always be done. It's never too late to start. It's never too late to heal.

Your childhood trauma affects your everyday life. It affects the relationships you build, your happiness, career, and your health. Your childhood was when you learned how to process each emotion, and when you add trauma to that equation, the way you process things may not be as healthy as you'd like it to be.

Think back to the times in your childhood when you felt unsafe, uncomfortable, and unhappy. If you have trouble uncovering these recollections but feel as though you can handle digging a bit deeper, try utilizing things from your past to jog your memory. This could be old photo albums, home videos, or even family stories.

Why Do We Have Suppressed Emotions?

Suppressed emotions are like silent sentinels of our past, standing guard over memories and experiences that were once too difficult, painful, or overwhelming to face. Particularly during childhood—a time when we are most vulnerable—the coping mechanisms we develop to handle these emotions can lead to suppression. As children, we might not have had the tools, the support, or simply the emotional capacity to process complex feelings, leading us to unconsciously push them down. This suppression, while protective at the moment, often comes at a cost that manifests later in our adult lives.

The Genesis of Suppressed Emotions

The origin of suppressed emotions typically lies in our childhood experiences. Known as inner child wounds, these are the deep psychological bruises we sustain during our earliest years. They often arise from experiences of neglect, abandonment, abuse, or misunderstanding. In an ideal world, a child would express their distress and find comfort in the understanding response of a caregiver. However, when a child's emotional expressions are ignored, dismissed, or punished, the child learns to suppress these feelings. They learn that expressing emotions does not lead to comfort but perhaps to more pain, isolation, or fear.

For instance, consider a child who cries over a broken toy and is scolded instead of consoled. The message received is not to show sadness or seek help but to internalize that feeling. Over time, this message becomes an ingrained habit—suppress rather than express.

Why We Push These Emotions Down

The reasons we push down emotions are multifaceted and deeply ingrained in our developmental psychology. One primary reason is the need for safety and acceptance. As children, our survival depends on our caregivers, making their acceptance critical. If showing vulnerability or distress leads to rejection, we suppress those parts of ourselves to maintain a bond with our caregivers.

Another reason is the lack of emotional skills. Children are not born knowing how to manage anger, sadness, or fear. These skills are ideally taught and modeled by adults. In their absence, children can conclude that their emotions must be hidden, a pattern that can solidify into adulthood.

Moreover, societal norms and expectations play a role. Many cultures teach children—particularly boys—that certain emotions such as fear or sadness are signs of weakness. The pressure to conform to these norms can lead a child to suppress emotions that are perfectly natural but deemed socially unacceptable.

The Consequences of Suppressed Emotions

When emotions are suppressed, they don't simply disappear. Instead, they can surface later as mood swings, anxiety, depression, or unexplained physical symptoms. In relationships, these suppressed emotions can lead to sensitivity to criticism, difficulty trusting others, or an inability to communicate effectively. Professionally, they might manifest as procrastination, a lack of motivation, or a fear of taking risks.

Suppressing emotions also prevents us from fully knowing ourselves. It disconnects us from our authentic feelings and needs, leading to a life that might feel unfulfilling or disconnected.

Healing the Wounds

Healing begins with recognition and validation of these suppressed emotions. This process involves revisiting our childhood experiences through the lens of compassion and understanding. Techniques like therapy, journaling, art, and mindfulness practices can help in acknowledging and processing these emotions.

Creating a dialogue with the inner child can be particularly healing. It involves imagining your younger self and mentally communicating with them—offering the understanding and support that was missing. This practice not only helps in healing old wounds but also in reclaiming the parts of ourselves lost to suppression.

Zarafshan Shiraz defines childhood trauma, in her article published in the Hindustan Times, as "anything that makes a child feel helpless or unsafe—like sexual, physical or verbal abuse, domestic violence, an unstable or unsafe environment; parental separation, neglect, bullying, a serious illness or invasive medical procedures" (Shiraz, 2022).

Shiraz (2022) highlights a few steps you can take to truly kickstart your healing process. They include:

- Acknowledging the problem and getting specific.
- Loving the child within you.
- Utilizing positive affirmations.
- Putting an end to negative self-talk.
- Learning from your internal wounds.

Acknowledging the problem and getting specific

By conducting a thorough examination of your life, you'll see patterns of behavior emerging. Follow those patterns back to the original memory or the root of the problem. At first, you might not want to accept that there is a problem at all. You believe that going through life without addressing your internal issues is the answer, but it isn't. Acceptance is the first step in true healing. The more you look at your life, what you've been through, and what you've grown from, the easier it will be to spot the hard times. Acknowledgement goes quite a long way, especially since your earliest years are the ones that shaped you into who you are today. Get specific about the events you experienced, understand the causes, and the triggers associated with it. Pinpoint the people involved, the environment in which you were in, and what roles they played in your trauma. When you're aware of your triggers and why you feel the way you do, you'll learn to let go of the past. You'll focus on your future instead.

Loving the child within you

It is essential to comfort your inner child through this process. Healing takes time, effort, and it can bring up a lot of pain that you may not have thought about in a long time. That little boy or girl you once were is still within you. They still need love and care to this day. Reconnecting with your inner child is loving them unconditionally. It's becoming the adult you wish you had when you were younger. What does your inner child feel? What do they need? There are times when you crave the simplicity of your childhood. You yearn for days that feel calm, that are filled with joy, despite the pain you may have endured then. A great way to integrate this back into your life is to do the things you loved to do as a kid. Even if they seem silly or pointless, know that they aren't. They're a part of how you heal. If you loved going outside in the afternoons to kick a ball around the backyard, do it. If you loved laying out under a tree in the park, do it. Play the games that made you happy, eat the snacks that lit up your day. Don't be afraid to lean into your playful side. Sometimes, that's exactly what you need.

Utilizing positive affirmations

The negative childhood events you experienced could've obstructed your brain pathways. They may have caused you to think negatively about yourself, especially if you grew up around people who always expected perfection.

My mother always made it a point to tell me everything I was doing wrong as a child, but never what I did right. I never did receive the satisfaction of having her tell me she was proud of me. All I got was her unmet, unrealistic expectations, and her clear disappointment. I was too young to understand, but I didn't have anyone there to tell me it was okay to make mistakes. I didn't know how damaging striving for perfection would be. I only did what I was told, and that took a toll on my self-esteem. As I got older, I realized just how much negative self-talk would rush through my mind every single day. Thoughts like, "your life is a mess and it's all your fault," and "you'll never be good enough. You're stressed because you can't do anything right. You'll never be able to get it together," took up so much space inside my head. Letting go of those thoughts and replacing them with kinder, optimistic ones completely transformed my life. It took me a while of consistently practicing positive affirmations to make me believe them, but once I did, it changed everything.

Putting an end to negative self-talk

Incorporating positive affirmations and thoughts is important to your mental health, but what do you do when the negative self-talk resurfaces? As you work on healing, you'll encounter a lot of difficult emotions that may feel hard to navigate. These emotions may cause the negative thoughts to emerge, making it hard for you to remember the positive ones. Learn to calm your mind when you feel overwhelmed, anxious, or stressed. If you find that the negative self-talk seems to be taking hold, combat it with relaxation techniques. You can try meditations, listening to podcasts or music, and reading to help ease the pressure you feel.

Learning from your internal wounds

Everything in life comes with a lesson. There is a lesson in every hardship you endure. At the start of my healing journey, I was afraid to learn from my adversities. I was afraid that it would somehow make things more difficult as I sought out to find the reasons behind my pain. I didn't want to be scared any longer. I didn't want to feel trapped and alone, stuck inside my mind. So, I decided in order to get the most out of my healing process, I needed to keep an open mind. I needed to work on separating the emotions from the memories, and study the memories themselves more closely. With that, I learned a lot about the person I am today. I understood how I got here and what I need to continue to grow.

Working to overcome your pain is no easy feat. Finding balance within yourself takes time. Be kind to yourself, be patient, and be open-minded. Your healing journey isn't linear. You're not supposed to have all of the answers right now, but with time, they'll all become apparent. All you have to do is be willing to try.

Healing Exercise

This exercise follows a simple technique to help you dismantle your negative thoughts and replace them with positive ones. First, I want you to set a timer for five minutes. Get into a comfortable position in a quiet room where you can be alone with your thoughts for the allotted time.

For those five minutes, you'll allow your negative thoughts to flow through your mind. Think of them as appearing one by one, waiting to be dismantled. Visualize each one disappearing and a positive thought taking its place. Remember, you may not believe your positive thoughts right away. They may feel disingenuous the first few times you do this exercise, but with practice, they'll stick.

Every time you feel weighed down by your thoughts, especially the negative self-talk, return to this exercise. Give yourself five minutes to get it all out, to replace the negativity with positivity, so you can focus on the good. Throughout your life, you'll see that there are enough people criticizing what you do. Don't join them. Don't be one of them. Build yourself up. Don't tear yourself down.

Heartfelt Reflections: A Journey Within

This reflective writing exercise is designed to guide you through a deep exploration of a moment when you felt inadequate or doubted your worth. It's an opportunity to closely examine these feelings, understand their origins, and learn how they influence your emotions and actions. This process is not just about recollection but about using these insights as a catalyst for personal growth and empowerment.treatment option for you.

Journal Prompt: Analyzing Feelings of Insufficiency

Think back to a recent time when you questioned your value or abilities. To fully engage with this reflection, follow these steps:

Identify the Incident: Recall the last instance when you felt that you weren't good enough. Where were you? What was happening?

_____

_____

_____

_____

_____

_____

_____

_____

Detail the Situation: Describe the events that led to these feelings of inadequacy. Who was involved? What specific actions or words triggered your self-doubt?

_____

_____

_____

_____

_____

_____

_____

_____

_____

Examine Your Emotions: Focus on the emotions you experienced during this moment. Were you hurt, angry, disappointed, or perhaps a mix of several feelings? Write about them in detail.

_____

_____

_____

_____

_____

_____

_____

_____

_____

_____

_____

_____

_____

Reflect on the Effects: Consider how this moment affected you. How did it influence your thoughts, decisions, or behavior thereafter?

_____

_____

_____

_____

_____

_____

_____

_____

_____

_____

_____

_____

_____

_____

_____

Context of Continued Growth

Your journey of self-reflection and healing has brought you to a point where your inner child has begun to heal and thrive through increased self-love and compassion. This progress stems from your conscious decision to prioritize your well-being and explore different pathways that might lead you out of feelings of stagnation. By choosing to heal your wounds, you've allowed yourself to move forward with greater awareness and openness.

Encouragement for Ongoing Healing

Continue this reflective practice regularly as there is no rush in the journey of self-discovery and healing. Each step you take, no matter how small, is a part of your broader path toward understanding and loving yourself more deeply. Allow these reflections to be a source of strength and transformation as you navigate your emotions and experiences with compassion and patience.

As you continue, remember that there is no timeline for this journey. Take it slow, put in the effort, and let your inner child shine.

There will be times you feel like your inner child did not receive the parenting they needed or deserved, but with the right tools you can actually reparent your inner child. Are you ready to move forward in this healing journey?

Chapter Four

RECONNECTING WITH AND REPARENTING THE CHILD INSIDE

All of us face the job of becoming a loving mother and father to our inner child.

—Margaret Paul

The childhood trauma you faced is part of the reason you feel so detached from your inner child. That trauma severed your connection and produced the kind of wounds that have stuck with you all of these years.

Have you given much thought to what could've caused your wounds? Allaya Cooks-Campbell's article, published on the *BetterUp Blog*, lists the different patterns of behavior that can help you identify whether your inner child is indeed wounded. They are:

- Frustration or irritation.
- Big reactions to unmet needs.
- Childish outbursts, like throwing tantrums or saying things you don't mean.
- Complaining that no one understands you or you don't feel heard.

- Difficulty explaining your feelings or why you're upset.
- Low self-esteem.
- A harsh inner critic.
- Immaturity.
- Patterns of self-sabotage.
- Fear of abandonment or commitment issues.
- Challenges with setting boundaries or expressing your needs (Cooks-Campbell, 2022).

As I navigated the complexities of early adulthood in my twenties, I began to recognize specific persistent patterns in my behavior and reactions. Initially, I dismissed these patterns as mere facets of my personality, seemingly ingrained and unchangeable. However, this perception dramatically shifted as I faced recurring challenges that illuminated the deeper issues at play.

During professional setbacks or interpersonal conflicts, I often found myself engulfed in despair. For example, a minor error at work would spiral into overwhelming anxiety about my competence. Similarly, expressing my feelings during stressful times with my partner was daunting—I struggled to articulate my emotions clearly. Each instance wasn't just situational discomfort but a manifestation of more profound, unresolved internal wounds.

My husband, noticing my distress, would frequently offer his support, asking what he could do to alleviate my anguish. "What can we do to fix the way you're feeling right now? What can I do to help?" His intentions were pure, yet his questions often left me feeling more isolated. I would freeze, shut down, and occasionally retort that he couldn't possibly understand my feelings—a statement stemming not from conviction but from my confusion about my emotional state.

These interactions underscored a fundamental truth: while the trials of adulthood added layers to my struggles, they were not the origin. The root lay much deeper, entangled with unresolved issues from my past. It was a rare day when I felt genuinely okay; frustration, irritation, and stress were my constant companions, and my low self-esteem was painfully evident. I tried recalling instances of confidence to lift my spirits, but these were fleeting and provided little solace.

Feeling utterly lost, I turned to inner child therapy, a decision that marked the beginning of a transformative journey. Through this therapeutic process, I realized the critical need to address and heal the wounds of my past to move forward. My goal became clear: I wanted to treat myself compassionately, listen attentively to my body's needs, and commit to nurturing my well-being.

As I progressed in therapy, I worked hard to visualize the little girl within me—the embodiment of my inner child, who needed care and understanding. Yet, visualizing was only the first step; the real challenge was translating these mental images into tangible actions that would genuinely improve my emotional health. It became evident that to truly connect with and heal my inner child, I had to learn how to put myself in her shoes—not just metaphorically, but in actions that reflected deep self-care and empathy. This realization was pivotal, guiding me toward a path where healing was not just a concept, but a lived daily experience.

Identifying Your Internal Wounds

Childhood trauma is a threat to your inner self or what psychology calls the "inner child." (Kapur, 2023). Your childhood trauma may be affecting you in ways you never thought possible. To think that every decision we make, every emotion we feel, and everything we do is somehow influenced by our childhood experience can be a lot to take in. Take it one step at a time. I'm here to guide you through the different causes of internal wounds so you can pinpoint your own.

Janvi Kapur describes these causes in her article published in *Sportskeeda*, which are:

- Emotional neglect.
- Lack of validation and appreciation.
- Off-hand comments.
- Invalidation.
- Violence (Kapur, 2023).

Let's dive deeper into each of these.

Emotional Neglect

Emotional neglect is not commonly recognized as child abuse, and often, it is not deliberate. Yet, the impact it has can leave deep and lasting scars. I invite you to reflect on your childhood: Did you ever feel like your emotions were overlooked by your parents? Were there times when you tried to express how you felt, only to find that your parents did not truly listen or understand?

Many parents, often without realizing it, may fail to address their child's emotional needs. They may be preoccupied with their own struggles or believe they are doing their best despite their shortcomings. This lack of attention to a child's emotional life can feel like neglect, leaving lasting impressions of being undervalued.

In my own experience, my mother was aware of my emotional state but chose to minimize its importance. She held the view that showing emotions was a sign of weakness. She encouraged me to suppress my feelings, insisting that ignoring them would make me stronger. This approach was often coupled with harsh criticism; she frequently called me "stupid" or "weak," chastising me for being emotional and urging me to "suck it up and be strong." Her words were meant to toughen me, but instead, they sowed seeds of doubt and anxiety in me.

As I grew older, despite my efforts to bury my emotions, they didn't vanish; they manifested as anxiety. It took a long time to understand that the harsh lessons imparted by my mother were not truths I had to live by but rather reflections of her limitations and fears.

Now, as you look back on your own experiences of emotional neglect, recognize that these moments were not your fault. It's crucial not to carry the weight of those negative memories. Allow yourself to feel the emotions you once had to push aside. Understand them, and then let them go. Feeling, understanding, and releasing is a vital step toward healing and reclaiming your emotional integrity.

Lack of Validation and Appreciation

Do you ever feel as though your parents or caregivers failed to recognize and value you during your childhood? Did they dismiss your feelings and also criticize the way you expressed them? Remember, as a child, you were primarily in a phase of learning, constantly observing the adults around you for cues and guidance to navigate and make sense of your emotions. Children are not inherently equipped with all the tools they need to fully understand and articulate their feelings, which underscores the critical role of parents in this developmental process.

In my upbringing, the sense of being undervalued was starkly evident. My mother and other family members frequently made it clear that they didn't fully appreciate my efforts. I was perpetually left feeling that no matter how hard I tried, it simply wasn't enough. This persistent lack of validation and appreciation likely didn't end in childhood but may have extended into your adult life as well. You might seek approval from friends, partners, or workplace superiors. The quest for validation often stems from the unmet emotional needs of your childhood.

However, one vital lesson to embrace is the power of self-appreciation. Acknowledging your achievements, regardless of their scale, can profoundly impact your self-esteem. Recognize and celebrate your progress and the obstacles you've overcome. There's much in your journey to take pride in. Holding onto this self-recognition is crucial—you don't necessarily need others' validation to feel confident and valued. Ultimately, the most enduring and empowering appreciation is what you offer yourself.

Offhand Comments

"What may be a life-changing sentence for a child, can very well be a regular Tuesday for the parent." (Kapur, 2023). This quote captures the profound impact seemingly casual remarks can have on a child. As children, we often look up to our parents for support, validation, and encouragement, eagerly wanting them to recognize our efforts and feel proud of us. However, offhand comments made without much thought by parents can leave deep-seated impressions.

Comments like, "I wish you were more like your brother," or "I'm ashamed of you" can echo in a child's mind long into adulthood. At a young age, processing such remarks is exceedingly difficult, especially when there's no follow-up apology or explanation from a parent to mitigate the words' impact. Such statements, perhaps delivered in moments of frustration or thoughtlessness, can significantly strain the parent-child relationship and severely dent a child's self-confidence.

For many, like myself, the realization of how these comments influenced various aspects of mental health only becomes apparent later in life. These words, once internalized, can frequently resurface, influencing our self-perception and everyday mental dialogues. The journey to unlearn these negative perceptions and reassess one's self-worth is often lengthy and challenging. It involves a deliberate effort to disbelieve the harmful assertions made during one's formative years and to view oneself objectively, recognizing and affirming one's potential and value independently of those early criticisms.

Invalidation

How often were you told as a child to stop crying or to stop being so dramatic? Were you ever dismissed by being told you had no reason to feel sad? My childhood frequently echoed with such dismissals. Although I was not prone to frequent outbursts and often sought solitude to cry, whenever my mother or other family members discovered me, my emotions were completely invalidated. They conveyed, whether intentionally or not, that my sadness or hurt was inappropriate, even though such feelings were perfectly normal.

This constant invalidation made me increasingly reluctant to seek comfort or support from my parents. The fear of triggering another painful argument or being further dismissed led me to isolate in times of distress. I would often retreat to a corner of my room, curling up until my tears subsided, so I could resume my daily life. This approach was far from healthy; it prevented me from truly processing my difficult emotions, teaching me instead to merely ignore them.

It's crucial to recognize that your emotions are valid and significant, regardless of how others may have dismissed them in the past. You should never feel the need to hide your feelings. Instead, it's important to learn to understand and express them healthily. Remember, acknowledging and addressing your emotions is a fundamental step toward healing and emotional resilience.

Violence

"Any form of violence can be a precursor to childhood trauma." (Kapur, 2023). Experiencing physical abuse when you're young harms more than just your body. It harms your mind. Parents may hit, push, or shove their children in the heat of the moment, returning to normal shortly after, believing that the child forgot, but they do not. Those moments stick with them. You don't have to experience violence yourself for it to have caused trauma. You could have witnessed things as a child that has affected you negatively. If you believe that you suffer from PTSD or you have severe trauma that you need to work through, don't be scared to reach out to a trained therapist. They're highly skilled and cautious when it comes to navigating such situations. Learning to ask for help is something that I struggled with when I got older, but it eventually dawned on me that I couldn't do it all alone. Healing internally does require a lot of reflection and patience, but it also requires support. You're not weak for asking for help. Finding support and relying on others takes more strength than you may realize.

There is a part of you that worries your wounds will never heal. You believe they're too deep, and you're too far gone to make any changes, but you'd be mistaken. No matter what stage of your life you're currently in, change is possible. You don't have to live with the pain of the past any longer. You don't have to burden yourself with the idea that your inner child is still in need of love. You have a chance to start again. You now have the opportunity to befriend that little child within.

Your Road to Reconnection

When I entered my twenties and the reality of adulthood finally hit me, I became obsessed with having my life together. Despite having to deal with anxiety, depression, and endless self-doubt, I wanted to appear like everything was fine. I tried my best to ignore the negativity floating around inside my mind until it became too much, and I realized that I was in desperate need of recalibration.

I felt like something was missing. I no longer had a sense of playfulness and imagination. I left all of that behind, convinced that it just wasn't the kind of thing I had time for, but that all changed during my healing journey. Facing painful memories and emotions was undoubtedly a significant part of the process, but I had forgotten how important it was to rebuild my connection with my inner child.

In Livia Boerger's article on *Made with Lemons*, she describes a few incredible strategies to reconnect. They are:

- Get messy.
- Treat yourself to something silly.
- Utilize a body scan meditation.
- Speak up for yourself.
- Reread a book from your childhood.
- Practice mindfulness.
- Get your feelings down on paper.
- Rekindle a childhood passion.
- Make time for daydreaming and visualization.
- Reconnect with old friends (Boerger, 2022).

Get Messy

Growing up, my parents always made it a point to scold me for making a mess. It didn't matter if it was just a few clothes on the edge of my bed or a book left on the floor after a reading session. They always perpetuated the idea of perfection; if I didn't fall in line, they'd be even more disappointed with me. I didn't have the chance to get messy as a kid and explore many things because I spent all of my time trying to get ahead. I was expected to be reading at higher levels and handling math problems that were far too complex for my age, all so I could succeed the way they wanted me to. As I revisited my childhood memories and began my reconnection, I made it a point to get messy. I let loose, picking up painting, spending time baking, and giving myself the freedom to be present. I didn't worry about the clean-up. I concentrated on fun the way I would've if I were still a child. Now is your time to explore and do the activities that will slowly heal your wounds. Focus on what makes you feel good. There will be plenty of time for tidying up later.

Speak Up for Yourself

Children usually don't have filters. They speak their mind and tell you exactly how they feel unless they're told to do otherwise. While having a filter as an adult is important, you must practice being honest with your feelings. Speak up for yourself when something bothers you, or you need time alone. I know what it's like to be a people-pleaser. I spent too much energy worrying about other people's opinions when I should've been putting myself first. Take care of your body and mind. Don't be afraid to say no, especially when saying yes compromises your mental, physical, and emotional health.

Reread a Book from Your Childhood

Children's books are filled with wonder, life lessons, and lovely messages to remember. I returned to my childhood home a few months after my first child was born. I hadn't been back in a few years and everything looked just like I remembered it. My mother never liked change and kept everything in its place, including my old books. Rereading some of my old favorites reminded me of the good times. I recalled being eager to crawl into bed early, so my mom could read them to me. This activity shook quite a few memories loose, and they reminded me how important it was to stay playful. The world can feel dull as we age, especially with all the responsibilities crowding our minds. A few simple stories may completely change your perspective. They might just allow you to dream big again.

Practice Mindfulness

Mindfulness is the practice of repeatedly focusing your awareness on the present moment (Hoshaw, 2022). By concentrating on your body's sensations, you'll gain a clearer understanding of your emotions without passing judgment. You don't need to criticize yourself for how you feel. Instead, pay closer attention to where the roots of those feelings are. Mindfulness allows you to make stronger connections to your childhood experience and uncover additional memories you may have suppressed.

Get Your Feelings Down on Paper

Journaling will become integral to your healing journey as you continue through this workbook and in your everyday life. Taking account of how you feel presently and giving yourself a space to explore the past is essential to making progress. You don't have to over-complicate the way you use your journal. You can spend a few minutes a day collecting your thoughts, writing down what you're grateful for, digging deeper into your current emotions, and exploring new ideas. When I was little, I loved writing stories in my journal. I would write the most interesting yet relatively simple narratives, and that process alone brought me so much joy. I started integrating more storytelling aspects into my everyday journaling sessions, which helped me connect with my inner child. Your journal is a safe place to share whatever is on your mind. Let it be your companion through this journey and every stage of your life.

Rekindle a Childhood Passion

I've revisited many of my childhood passions by spending time with my kids. I watched how they became fascinated by bugs in the backyard, how they made new games when tired of the old ones, and how they'd eat their popsicles on a hot summer afternoon. They never gave much thought about being covered in dirt or the remnants of their frozen treats. They were simply happy to be there, enjoying every minute of playtime.

Make Time for Daydreaming and Visualization

Start by setting aside quiet moments in your day, moments when you can be alone with your thoughts without interruptions. It could be early morning as the sun rises or late at night when the world has quieted. Find a comfortable space where you can relax and let your guard down. As you settle into this space, allow yourself to daydream. Visualize scenarios where you feel safe, loved, and happy. Imagine your inner child in these scenes—what are they doing? Perhaps they're playing freely in a sunlit meadow or curled up with a book in a cozy, hidden nook.

Engage with these visualizations actively. Introduce elements that bring joy and comfort to your inner child. Maybe it's the gentle touch of a breeze, the laughter of friends, or the soothing presence of a kind, understanding figure. Whatever these elements are, use them to build a sanctuary in your mind, a place where your inner child can thrive and feel valued.

This practice of daydreaming isn't about escapism; it's a way to rewire old memories, giving your inner child the nurturing and care they missed. Over time, these positive visualizations can help reshape how you view yourself, fostering a sense of peace and self-acceptance that heals old wounds. As you reconnect with your inner child through visualization, you gradually restore the joy and innocence that were always yours to claim.

Reconnect with Old Friends

Revisiting relationships with friends from your past can serve as a unique bridge to access memories and feelings that are vital parts of your inner child. These friends often hold keys to our forgotten happiness, the unguarded laughter, the shared secrets, and the carefree adventures that characterized our youth. They remind us of who we were before life's disappointments and responsibilities began to shape our self-perception and actions.

Start by reaching out with a simple message or call. It might feel awkward initially, especially if much time has passed, but remember that genuine connections can rekindle from even the tiniest ember of warmth. Share your current journey with them; you might find that they, too, have been longing for connection and healing. This exchange can reignite old bonds and create new memories.

As you engage with these friends, allow yourself to reminisce about the days you spent together. Discuss the dreams you once shared, the challenges you've faced, and the growth you've both experienced. Such conversations are not just nostalgic; they are therapeutic, enabling you to reconnect with parts of yourself that you might have forgotten or neglected.

Moreover, seeing yourself through the eyes of someone who knew you in simpler times can be incredibly affirming. It can dismantle the harsh judgments you've imposed on yourself over the years. This perspective helps heal the wounds of your inner child by reinforcing the notion that you were, and still are, worthy of love, friendship, and happiness.

Through this reconnection, not only do you revisit the essence of your early experiences, but you also weave them into the fabric of your current identity, helping your inner child feel seen and valued once more. This process doesn't just mend old wounds—it enriches your present life, adding depth and warmth to your ongoing narrative.

Reparenting Your Inner Child

The concept of the "inner child" is more than just a psychological buzzword—it's a profound aspect of who we are, encapsulating the purest emotions and experiences from our earliest years. This part of us influences our adult behavior and relationships, often more than we realize.

Think of the inner child as the emotional DNA that shapes how we respond to the world. For instance, feelings of being overlooked in group settings or relationships can often be traced back to moments in childhood when we felt neglected. I remember moments from childhood when I felt invisible during family gatherings, which I've carried into adulthood, often feeling the same in social situations.

Recognizing when this part of you needs attention is crucial for emotional health. Signs might include unexplained sadness, irritability, or a pervasive sense of insecurity in stable relationships. These are indications that the inner child within might be hurt and seeking your attention.

By acknowledging and nurturing our inner child, we can address these deep-seated emotions and begin to heal. This understanding of your inner child isn't just about looking back—it's about growing forward, allowing ourselves to find joy and security in our present lives.

The Significance of Reparenting

Reparenting is a journey back to the younger version of yourself, who might have missed out on certain emotional support. This process involves giving yourself the love, attention, and guidance you needed but didn't receive during your early years. It's about being the nurturing parent to yourself that you always needed. Reparenting isn't just about revisiting the past; it's about changing how you react to it today, providing the comfort and support that were missing.

Think of reparenting as stepping into the role of a wise and compassionate parent for yourself. It's a way to heal old wounds by actively rewriting the emotional blueprints from your childhood. These blueprints, crafted during your formative years, influence how you view the world, interact with others, and, most importantly, how you see yourself. If these were built on unstable grounds—perhaps through neglect or misunderstanding—reparenting helps you to rebuild them on a foundation of self-acceptance and understanding.

Why is this important? For starters, many of us carry forward the echoes of past criticisms that continue to shape our self-image and interactions. If you grew up in an environment where showing emotion was discouraged, for example, you might struggle to form close relationships or express your feelings. Reparenting teaches you to honor and express your emotions appropriately, which is essential for building strong, healthy connections.

Boosting your self-esteem is another crucial aspect of reparenting. Imagine transforming the critical inner voice that says you're not good enough into one that supports and believes in you. This change doesn't just help you feel better about yourself; it empowers you to embrace life's opportunities more fully.

Practical Steps for Reparenting Your Inner Child

Here are practical steps to guide you through this deeply rewarding journey.

1. Recognizing the Needs of Your Inner Child

Your inner child's needs can often be masked by adult responsibilities and rationalizations. Identify moments when you feel particularly vulnerable, reactive, or anxious. These emotions may indicate that your inner child is calling out for attention. Pay close attention to patterns in your emotional responses—do certain situations trigger feelings of insecurity or inadequacy? These can provide clues to the needs of your inner child.

2. Connecting with Your Inner Child

Several exercises can help you connect more deeply with your inner child.

- Journaling: Use a journal to communicate directly with your inner child. Write out what you feel and ask your inner child what they need from you right now. The act of journaling can reveal deep-seated emotions and help you understand your inner child better.

- Meditation: Meditation can be a powerful tool for self-reflection and connection. Try guided meditations that focus on healing and nurturing your inner self.
- Reflective Questioning: Ask yourself questions like, "What did I need as a child that I didn't get?" "When do I feel most like my younger self?" and "What makes my inner child feel safe?" These questions can uncover profound insights into your past and present emotional needs.

3. Creating a Safe Emotional Space

Your inner child needs a safe emotional environment to heal. A safe emotional environment involves physically and emotionally making space where you can be vulnerable and reflective. It might mean setting up a small area in your home where you feel comfortable and can be undisturbed, or it could be a mental space you enter through visualization or meditation.

4. Offering Comfort and Reassurance

To soothe and reassure your inner child, practice using positive affirmations that affirm your value, strength, and worth. Phrases like "I am loved," "I am capable," and "I am worthy of good things" can be powerful. Visualization can also play a role here; imagine comforting your younger self, giving them the compassion and understanding they need.

5. Establishing Healthy Boundaries and Coping Strategies

Learning to set boundaries is crucial in reparenting. Establishing boundaries means learning to say no to others when you are overextended and yes to your own needs. Develop new coping strategies that support healthy emotional regulation. For instance, if you feel overwhelmed, instead of succumbing to old patterns of behavior, you might choose to take a walk, practice deep breathing, or reach out to a supportive friend.

6. Integrating Playfulness and Joy

Often, we forget to incorporate joy and playfulness into our adult lives. Allow yourself to explore activities that bring you joy or revisit hobbies you loved as a child. Integrating playfulness can include anything from painting and dancing to playing a sport or watching favorite childhood movies. These activities can significantly lighten your emotional load and bring a sense of renewal.

7. The Importance of Patience and Consistency

The journey of reparenting is not linear. It requires patience and consistency, as old wounds can take time to heal, and growth can be gradual. Regularly engaging in these practices, even when challenging, helps reinforce your commitment to healing and assures your inner child that they are important and cared for.

Remember, reparenting is a profound act of self-love. It's not just about healing the past but empowering your present and future. Embrace this journey with an open heart, and watch as you transform your relationship with yourself and the world around you.

Navigating Challenges in Reparenting

One of the most common obstacles in reparenting is encountering deep-seated resistance within yourself. This resistance often manifests when revisiting painful memories or confronting long-held beliefs about yourself. It might feel easier to avoid these uncomfortable feelings rather than face them head-on. Additionally, life's daily stresses and responsibilities can distract from your reparenting work, making it easy to deprioritize your healing journey.

To overcome these obstacles, it's crucial to set aside dedicated time for your reparenting practice. Navigating these challenges could mean scheduling regular intervals—daily or weekly—where you focus solely on nurturing your inner child. It's also helpful to integrate reparenting into your daily routine in smaller ways, like starting each day with a positive affirmation that supports your inner child.

Resistance can also come directly from your inner child, particularly if the wounds are deep and the trust in adult figures is severely compromised. Your inner child may fear the vulnerability that comes with opening up and re-experiencing the pain.

When you sense resistance, it's important to approach your inner child with compassion rather than frustration. Acknowledge the fear or discomfort openly and provide reassurance that you can now provide the safety and love that was missing. Techniques such as dialoguing with your inner child through journaling can help break through this resistance. Writing a letter from your adult self to your inner child, detailing how you will protect and cherish them, can be particularly effective.

While many aspects of reparenting can be self-guided, there are times when professional help is necessary. If you find yourself overwhelmed by the emotions that arise, or if you notice that your mental health is deteriorating rather than improving, it may be time to seek therapy or counseling.

Professional therapists can offer guidance that is informed by psychological training and experience. They provide a safe space to explore your feelings and can introduce coping strategies that might not be accessible alone. Moreover, therapists can help you navigate the complex emotions that reparenting stirs up and can support you in developing effective ways to communicate with and soothe your inner child.

Exploring different types of therapy can also be beneficial. Cognitive-behavioral therapy (CBT) is effective for changing harmful thinking patterns. Meanwhile, psychodynamic therapy focuses on understanding emotional blind spots by examining past experiences. For a more holistic approach, integrative therapy combines elements from different methods tailored to your needs.

Incorporating group therapy or support groups where others are engaged in similar journeys can also provide encouragement and reduce feelings of isolation. Hearing others' experiences can validate your own and provide new perspectives on your healing process.

Healing Exercises

Preparation:

Find a quiet, comfortable space where you won't be interrupted. You might want to create a soothing environment with items that make you feel safe, such as soft blankets, gentle lighting, or calming music. Have a journal or paper and a pen nearby to record any insights or feelings that arise.

Step 1: Visualization

Close your eyes and take a few deep breaths to center yourself. Imagine a place that feels utterly safe and comforting to you. Visualize your inner child in this place. See them clearly—their age, expressions, and body language. Notice what they are doing and how they seem to feel.

Step 2: Approach with Compassion

In your visualization, approach your inner child slowly and with kindness. Greet them warmly and sit with them. Observe their reactions to your presence. It's important to be patient; your inner child may initially be wary or afraid.

Step 3: Open Dialogue

Begin a conversation with your inner child. You can start by asking simple questions like:

- How are you feeling today?
- What do you need right now?
- Is there something you'd like to tell me?
- Listen attentively to their responses. Remember, communication can be nonverbal too, so pay attention to gestures and emotions.

Step 4: Offer Reassurance

Reassure your inner child that you are there to protect and care for them. Offer comforting words or gestures that you feel you needed when you were that age. You might say things like:

- "I am here for you now."
- "It's okay to feel sad or scared, I'm here to help you through it."
- "You are loved and valued just as you are."

Step 5: Engage in a Healing Activity

Engage your inner child in an activity that they find enjoyable or comforting. It could be imagining playing a game, reading a story together, or simply sitting quietly. This step is about creating joyful, comforting experiences for your inner child.

Step 6: Make a Commitment

Before concluding the visualization, make a commitment to your inner child. Promise them that you will continue to be there for them, to listen to them, and to meet their needs. Affirm that you are committed to nurturing and protecting them.

Step 7: Reflection

Gradually bring yourself back to the present. Open your eyes when you're ready and take a few deep breaths. Reflect on the experience and write down any insights, emotions, or commitments from your exercise in your journal. This will help reinforce your intentions and the healing process.

Regular Practice

Repeat this exercise regularly, ideally as part of a daily or weekly routine. Each session can help reinforce the sense of safety and love, gradually healing old wounds and changing how you relate to yourself.

This reparenting exercise can be profoundly healing, helping to foster a nurturing relationship with yourself that perhaps was lacking in your childhood. By consistently showing up for your inner child, you teach your adult self how to care for your deepest needs.

Heartfelt Reflections: A Journey Within

As you delve into the process of reconnecting with and reparenting your inner child, these prompts are intended to facilitate deep introspection and foster a nurturing dialogue between you and the younger self residing within.

Prompt 1: Meeting Your Inner Child

Imagine a quiet, safe place where you can meet your inner child. Visualize this scene in detail. What does this place look like? What sounds do you hear? As you approach your inner child, what expression do they have? Begin your journal entry by describing this meeting. Write down what you would say to your inner child, and imagine what they might say to you in return.

_____

_____

_____

_____

_____

_____

_____

_____

_____

_____

_____

Prompt 2: Acknowledging the Pain

Reflect on a moment from your childhood when you felt misunderstood, scared, or alone. Write about this memory from your current perspective. Offer words of comfort to your inner child about this moment. How can you validate their feelings now? What understanding can you provide that wasn't available then?

_____

_____

_____

_____

_____

_____

_____

_____

_____

_____

_____

_____

Prompt 3: Celebrating the Joyful Moments

It's also vital to recall moments of joy and triumph. Think of a happy, carefree moment from your childhood. Describe this memory in vivid detail—consider the sights, sounds, and smells accompanying it. How did you feel at that moment? Write a letter from your adult self to your child self, celebrating this joyful experience.

_____

_____

_____

_____

_____

_____

_____

_____

_____

_____

_____

_____

_____

_____

_____

Prompt 4: Building Trust

Reparenting involves building trust with your inner child. Write about how you can build this trust. What promises do you want to make to your inner child? How can you show them they can rely on you to be the caring, protective figure they need?

_____

_____

_____

_____

_____

_____

_____

_____

_____

_____

_____

_____

_____

_____

_____

_____

_____

Prompt 5: Envisioning the Future Together

Finally, look forward. What dreams or goals do you have for yourself and your inner child? Describe how you can work together to achieve these aspirations. What steps will you take to ensure your inner child feels heard and valued along this journey?

_____

_____

_____

_____

_____

_____

_____

_____

_____

_____

_____

_____

_____

_____

_____

_____

_____

_____

_____

_____

Through these reflective journaling exercises, you are acknowledging and healing past wounds and paving the way for a future where your inner child and adult self walk hand in hand, empowered and whole. This journey within is not just about looking back—it's about moving forward with compassion and strength.

Many people have a hard time forgiving themselves and others for the trauma of our past. The next chapter is all about learning to embrace forgiveness and compassion in all aspects. Let's jump right in!

Chapter Five

EMBRACING FORGIVENESS, NURTURING COMPASSION, AND FINDING RELEASE

To forgive is to set a prisoner free and discover that the prisoner was you.

—Lewis B. Smedes

Forgiveness is often seen as a gift to another, but when directed inward, it can be incredibly liberating and transformative, especially when healing one's inner child. The inner child holds onto all the emotional memories of our past—the hurts, disappointments, and fears we encountered during our formative years. Without forgiveness, these memories can create emotional burdens that linger into adulthood, shaping our self-perception and reactions in ways we might not even be aware of.

Forgiving ourselves helps to release these burdens. It involves understanding and accepting that we did the best we could with the knowledge and resources we had at the time. Forgiveness doesn't mean condoning past mistakes or harmful behaviors but viewing them with compassion and context. By doing so, we allow ourselves to move past self-criticism and guilt, which are barriers to personal growth and happiness.

The act of forgiveness also rewrites the narratives we hold about ourselves. It replaces feelings of unworthiness and inadequacy with a narrative of growth and resilience. This shift is crucial because it affects how we approach current challenges and future opportunities. When we're not weighed down by past regrets or harsh self-judgments, we have more emotional energy to invest in building a fulfilling life.

Moreover, forgiveness opens the door to more profound emotional healing. It soothes the inner child who still feels the pain of past experiences, offering reassurance that they are worthy of love and belonging despite their imperfections. This nurturing approach can dramatically shift our internal landscape from harshness to support and encouragement.

Understanding Forgiveness and Its Impact on the Inner Child

Understanding the profound impact of forgiveness, particularly concerning our inner child, invites us into a deeper exploration of the psychology underpinning it. Forgiveness, often misconstrued as a mere interpersonal gesture, transcends the boundaries of reconciling with others to touch the core of our being—our inner child. This inner child, the echo of our younger selves, harbors the raw emotions and memories that shaped who we have become.

From a psychological standpoint, forgiveness is an act of consciously releasing resentment, anger, or the desire for vengeance, regardless of whether the perceived wrongdoing is excused. In the context of the inner child, this process becomes especially crucial. The grievances we carry from childhood, if unresolved, can seep into our adult lives, manifesting as persistent feelings of bitterness and mistrust that shadow our interactions and self-perception.

Why is this release necessary? Unresolved anger and resentment are like chains that bind us to the past. For the inner child, these emotions can be particularly damaging. When children experience hurt, they do not possess the full emotional capabilities to process these feelings logically. Instead, they may internalize the pain, leading to deep-seated emotional wounds that carry into adulthood. This unresolved emotional baggage can stifle growth and lead to a pervasive sense of unhappiness and dissatisfaction.

By choosing forgiveness, we do not negate or diminish the significance of our childhood experiences. Instead, we acknowledge and validate our feelings and consciously decide to let those grievances go. This decision is less about condoning past hurts and more about refusing to allow them to control our current emotional state. It's an act of reclaiming power over our emotional well-being.

The impact of holding onto anger is equally profound. Neurologically, when we dwell on negative emotions, we strengthen the neural pathways associated with them, which makes them more predominant in our emotional landscape. Holding onto these emotions can lead to heightened anxiety, depression, and a pervasive sense of insecurity. For the inner child whose emotional responses are raw and exposed, the effects are compounded. These compounded emotions can manifest as an adult who feels perpetually stuck or unable to move forward in various aspects of life, from personal relationships to professional environments.

48

Therefore, forgiveness is transformative. It involves re-narrating our story so we are no longer victims of our past but survivors who choose to heal and grow. Forgiveness doesn't happen overnight. It requires patience, repeated affirmations, and continuous self-reflection. As we practice forgiveness, we gradually dissolve the old pathways of resentment and create new ones filled with hope and renewal.

Forgiving ourselves is perhaps the most challenging yet rewarding part of this journey. It requires us to look inward with compassion and understand that our mistakes, whether as children or adults, do not define our worth. By forgiving ourselves, we heal our inner child, soothing the past pains and reassuring that part of ourselves that it is loved, valued, and worthy.

In essence, forgiveness is the key to emotional freedom. It liberates the inner child from the weight of past pains and opens up a space for new growth and happiness. This process allows us to become a more mature, fulfilled version of ourselves, where our past does not hold us back but propels us forward. Through understanding and practicing forgiveness, we not only heal our inner child but set the stage for a life rich with compassion and resilience.

Healing Exercise

Preparation:
Find a quiet, comfortable space where you will not be disturbed. You may choose to light a candle or use soft lighting to create a soothing atmosphere. Have some paper and a pen ready for parts of the exercise, and perhaps keep comforting objects or images nearby.

Step 1: Grounding
Sit comfortably and close your eyes. Take several deep, slow breaths to center yourself. Feel the weight of your body supported by the ground or chair, allowing tension to melt away with each exhale.

Step 2: Reflection
Open your eyes and begin by writing down a specific incident from your past where you feel you made a mistake or were not your best self. Describe the situation briefly, focusing on your actions and feelings at the time.

Step 3: Understanding
Close your eyes again, and imagine your inner child experiencing the same situation. Try to understand the circumstances from a child's perspective. Consider what needs you were trying to meet, even if the method was flawed. Recognize the limitations and the knowledge you had at that time.

Step 4: Dialogue

Write a dialogue between your adult self and your inner child about this incident. Allow your inner child to express any feelings of hurt, disappointment, or confusion, and respond with your adult wisdom, compassion, and understanding. This can be a powerful moment to acknowledge the pain and validate the feelings without judgment.

Step 5: Offer Forgiveness

Still in your dialogue, have your adult self offer forgiveness to your inner child. You might say something like:

- "I forgive you for the mistakes you made; you were doing the best you could with what you knew."
- "You are worthy of love and compassion, no matter your past actions."
- "I release you from the guilt and shame of this memory."

Step 6: Embrace and Reassure

Imagine embracing your inner child, providing comfort and reassurance. Feel the emotional release that comes with forgiveness. Affirm that you are both worthy of moving forward without the burden of past mistakes.

Step 7: Commit to Compassion

Conclude this exercise by committing to treat yourself with kindness and understanding moving forward. Write a commitment statement such as, "I commit to treating myself with the same compassion and forgiveness that I offer others."

Step 8: Closure

Gently bring your focus back to the present. Take a few deep breaths, and when you feel ready, open your eyes. Keep the writings from this exercise in a safe place where you can revisit them if feelings of self-blame resurface.

Regular Practice

Consider repeating this exercise periodically, especially when feelings of guilt or shame about past actions arise. Each session can deepen the healing and reinforce the habit of self-compassion and forgiveness.

This exercise helps integrate the understanding that everyone makes mistakes and that these do not diminish our worth or our capacity to give and receive love.

The Role of Compassion in Self-Forgiveness

In the intricate dance of human emotions, self-compassion is a step many of us miss, especially regarding self-forgiveness. Self-compassion is not just a buzzword; it's a fundamental practice that challenges us to treat ourselves with the same kindness and understanding that we might offer to a good friend in distress.

What Is Self-Compassion?

Self-compassion is an embracing attitude toward oneself that involves recognizing one's suffering, acknowledging it without judgment, and responding with kindness and care. It is rooted in the idea that all humans are imperfect and vulnerable. These qualities do not diminish our worth but are essential aspects of our shared human experience.

When we practice self-compassion, we shift from a mindset of criticism and isolation to one of warmth and shared humanity. We begin to see our flaws and mistakes not as damning evidence of inadequacy but as part of the imperfect tapestry of human life. This perspective doesn't just reshape our view of ourselves; it can fundamentally alter how we engage with the world.

Techniques for Developing Self-Compassion

Developing self-compassion can be transformative, yet it does require intentional practice. Here are some strategies that can help you cultivate a compassionate relationship with yourself:

- **Practice Gratitude:** Incorporating gratitude with self-compassion can enhance feelings of well-being by shifting focus from what's lacking or perceived as wrong to appreciating what is present and right. A daily gratitude journal can be a practical tool for writing down what you're thankful for and acknowledging and thanking yourself for the steps you've taken to care for your well-being.

- **Set Compassionate Goals:** Often, our goals are framed in the language of shoulds and musts, which can create unnecessary pressure. Try setting goals from a place of self-compassion. For example, instead of setting a goal like "I must lose weight," consider framing it as "I want to nurture my body with healthy food and more movement because I deserve to feel good."

- **Communicate Compassionately with Others:** As self-compassion grows, it naturally influences how you interact with others. Compassionate communication involves listening

actively, speaking kindly, and offering empathy. Compassionate communication not only improves your relationships but also reinforces your internal practice of compassion, creating a feedback loop that strengthens both.

- **Create Compassionate Routines:** Integrate self-compassion into your daily routines. Compassionate routines might look like starting your day with a self-compassion meditation, taking moments for deep breathing during work, or ending your day with a self-appreciation ritual. These practices help cement self-compassion as a daily habit.

As self-compassion becomes a way of life, its transformative impact is profound. Individuals who consistently practice self-compassion report higher levels of happiness and motivation, coupled with lower levels of anxiety and depression. Self-compassion provides a buffer against the harsh self-criticism that can often hinder us.

Moreover, self-compassion encourages us to accept and love ourselves as we are, which paradoxically opens us up to initiating positive changes. When we feel accepted and loved, we are more confident and secure, providing a stable foundation from which we can grow. It's not about being complacent, but about recognizing that growth comes more effectively from a place of acceptance than from a place of inadequacy.

Steps to Forgiving Others

Forgiving others, particularly those who have contributed to the wounds of our inner child, is one of the most challenging yet transformative aspects of our emotional healing journey. This process is not about condoning hurtful behaviors or dismissing our pain but about freeing ourselves from resentment and bitterness. When we choose to forgive, we take a profound step toward personal peace and healing reverberating throughout our lives.

Understanding the Nature of Forgiveness

Forgiveness is an act of strength and compassion. It involves acknowledging the pain caused by others but deciding that this pain will no longer affect your emotional well-being. Forgiveness does not mean forgetting the hurt or pretending it never happened. Instead, it means consciously releasing the anger and resentment that tie your energy to the past. This decision often requires a deep understanding of human flaws and a commitment to your emotional liberation.

Steps to Fostering Forgiveness

- **Acknowledge the Hurt:** Begin by fully acknowledging the harm done without minimization or exaggeration. Recognize how these actions impacted your life and let feelings of betrayal, sadness, or anger surface. Honesty with yourself is crucial in this initial step.

- **Empathize with the Offender:** Empathizing can be one of the most challenging steps, but it's often pivotal. Try to see the situation from the other person's perspective. Consider their limitations, their possible hurt, and how these factors might have influenced their behaviors. Empathy does not excuse the behavior but can help you understand it, which is often a key to finding forgiveness.

- **Decide to Forgive:** Forgiveness is a choice, often a difficult one. It's important to decide internally to let go of the resentment. This decision might not bring immediate emotional relief, but it sets your healing process in motion.

- **Communicate Your Forgiveness:** This step is optional and depends on your situation. Sometimes, directly telling the person that you forgive them can be therapeutic. In other cases, mainly where there is a risk of further emotional harm, this communication might be a letter that you do not send or a symbolic conversation in your mind.

- **Release the Bitterness:** Releasing bitterness can involve rituals or symbolic acts, such as writing your resentment on paper and burning it. These acts can signify your decision to let go of the anger and pain.

- **Embrace Healing and Growth:** Once you have decided to forgive, focus on what this opens up for you. Engage in activities that nurture your growth and healing. Cultivate positivity through new experiences, relationships, and personal achievements.

The Healing Benefits of Releasing Bitterness and Blame

The decision to release bitterness and blame is profoundly healing. Emotionally, it can lift the heavy weight of resentment that may have been consuming a significant amount of your mental and emotional energy. Letting go frees up this energy for more constructive and fulfilling pursuits.

Physiologically, forgiveness has been linked to better heart health, reduced stress, and improved immunity. Holding onto anger and resentment can trigger the body's stress response, leading to a variety of health issues. Releasing these can help restore your body's balance and improve overall well-being (Hopkins Medicine, 2021).

Socially, forgiveness can transform your relationships. It can lead to deeper connections, as you develop a greater capacity for empathy and understanding. Even if the relationships that caused the hurt do not survive, your ability to interact with others in a healthier, more open way is enhanced (Hopkins Medicine, 2021).

Integrating forgiveness into your life is about embracing a perspective that looks forward to possibilities rather than backward at pain. The process will not be linear or quick. Each step toward forgiveness requires patience and self-compassion. However, the journey, while challenging, is incredibly rewarding. It paves the way not just for healed relationships and inner peace but for a new chapter in your life where you can live more freely, connect to the present, and be optimistic about the future.

Steps to Forgiving Yourself

Integrating forgiveness into our daily lives is much like cultivating a garden; it requires patience, nurturing, and regular attention. It's a continuous practice that enhances our well-being and enriches our interactions. Maintaining a forgiving and compassionate mindset fosters an environment where healing can flourish, impacting ourselves and those around us.

Forgiveness as a Daily Practice

The concept of forgiveness often feels monumental, reserved for moments of great betrayal or pain. However, the essence of forgiveness can—and should—be woven into the fabric of our everyday lives. Forgiveness begins with the understanding that forgiveness is not a one-off act or a grand gesture but a series of small choices and practices that, over time, shape our emotional landscape.

- **Start with Self-Talk:** Our inner dialogue significantly influences our perception of the world and ourselves. To cultivate a forgiving mindset, observe how you talk to yourself throughout the day. When you make a mistake or fall short of your expectations, what do you say to yourself? Is your self-talk harsh, critical, or unforgiving? Practice replacing these thoughts with more compassionate and understanding responses. Instead of thinking, "I can't believe I messed up again," try, "Everyone makes mistakes. What can I learn from this?"

- **Embrace Mindful Moments:** Mindfulness can help anchor forgiveness in your daily routine. It involves being present in the moment and accepting it without judgment. This practice can be beneficial when feelings of anger or resentment arise. By noticing these feelings without immediately reacting, you give yourself space to choose how to respond, often leading to more forgiving and compassionate outcomes.

- **Cultivate Gratitude:** Gratitude and forgiveness are deeply interconnected. By regularly acknowledging and appreciating what you have, you can shift your focus away from grievances and toward positivity. Keep a gratitude journal, and each day, write down three things you are thankful for. This habit boosts your mood and makes forgiving easier, as it puts the grievances into perspective.

- **Set Intentions for Forgiveness:** Each morning, set an intention to forgive throughout the day. These intentions could be as simple as reminding yourself to be kind to everyone you interact with, including yourself, or it could involve setting a specific goal like, "Today, I will let go of a grudge I've been holding onto." Setting intentions helps to prime your mind to respond with forgiveness in situations where you might not naturally do so.

- **Practice Empathy:** Try to see situations from other people's perspectives. Empathy doesn't just reduce conflict—it enhances your ability to forgive. When someone irritates or hurts you, consider their circumstances or possible reasons behind their actions. Understanding others' motivations and struggles can make it easier to forgive them.

- **Create Reconciliation Rituals:** Sometimes, integrating forgiveness into your life means taking active steps toward reconciliation. These rituals might involve writing letters (sent or unsent), initiating conversations, or simply deciding to move forward in a relationship with a new understanding. Remember, reconciliation does not mean condoning hurtful behavior; it means resolving not to let past actions control your future happiness.

Forgiveness as a Lifestyle

Ultimately, integrating forgiveness into your daily life means adopting it as a lifestyle—a continuous commitment to viewing the world and your experiences through empathy, compassion, and grace. This lifestyle fosters resilience, allowing you to bounce back from setbacks and disappointments with a stronger, more compassionate outlook.

Living a life rooted in forgiveness also means embracing imperfection—in yourself and others. Recognizing that no one is infallible allows for a more realistic and gracious interaction with the world. It encourages a culture of forgiveness that can extend beyond personal interactions to influence broader societal attitudes.

Enduring Impact of a Forgiving Mindset

The benefits of a forgiving mindset extend beyond immediate emotional relief. They contribute to long-term health and happiness, enhancing physical health, deepening relationships, and fostering a robust emotional resilience capable of withstanding life's challenges. More importantly, a forgiving mindset allows for continuous personal growth and learning. It opens up a space where mistakes are seen as opportunities for growth, and personal setbacks are viewed with kindness and understanding.

As you continue to cultivate forgiveness in your daily life, remember that each step forward enriches not only your life but also the lives of those around you. Forgiveness is not just about overcoming past pains—it's about building a future characterized by emotional generosity and peace. This transformative practice reshapes not only how you interact with the past but also how you envision and create your future.

Embracing Forgiveness: Exercises

As you journey through the process of forgiveness, particularly in the context of healing your inner child and mending past relationships, it is beneficial to engage in practical exercises that allow you to apply what you have learned. These exercises are designed to deepen your understanding of forgiveness and to make this abstract concept a tangible part of your daily life. Let's dive into these practices with an open heart and a committed spirit, ready to transform insights into actions.

Exercise 1: Write a Forgiveness Letter to Your Inner Child

Often, we may not realize while growing up and facing life's demands, we have inadvertently neglected or silenced our inner child—the most vulnerable and genuine part of ourselves. This exercise is a profound step toward making amends with that part of you.

Start by finding a quiet, comfortable space where you won't be disturbed. Take a few deep breaths to center yourself. With a pen and paper in hand, begin your letter:

- First, acknowledge the times you might have ignored or overlooked the needs of your inner child. Be specific about the instances you remember or the general behaviors you exhibited that might have contributed to this neglect.
- Express genuine regret for these actions and the pain they may have caused. It's important to validate the feelings of your inner child, letting them know that their emotions are understood and respected.
- Offer assurances of change. Describe how you are working to be more attentive and nurturing toward your inner child. Commit to listening more, caring deeply, and responding to their needs.
- End the letter with a statement of forgiveness, asking for it from your inner child and offering it to yourself. Recognize that healing is a process, and both of you are learning and growing together.

This letter is for you and your inner child alone—it's a personal artifact of your healing journey, a testament to your commitment to growth and self-compassion.

Exercise 2: Forgive a Past Hurt Involving Someone Else

Think of a past incident where someone hurt you, which still triggers negative feelings when you recall it. This exercise involves applying the steps of forgiveness to this memory.

- Begin by clearly articulating the incident. Write down what happened and how it made you feel. This acknowledgment is crucial as it confronts the pain head-on.
- Next, attempt to understand the situation from the other person's perspective. Consider their circumstances, possible limitations, or stresses that might have influenced their behavior. Remember, understanding their motives is not about excusing their actions but about seeing the context in which they occurred.
- Decide to forgive. This decision might not lead to immediate emotional resolution, but it sets the intention to heal and move forward.
- Reflect on this forgiveness process. How has your perspective on the event changed? Do you feel a sense of release or peace? How does this act of forgiveness help you grow?

Exercise 3: Daily Mindfulness Practice Focused on Compassion

Mindfulness and compassion are intertwined qualities that, when practiced regularly, can significantly enhance your emotional well-being and relationships.

- Dedicate a few minutes each day to practice mindfulness. You can start by focusing on your breath, noticing the sensations of breathing in and out.
- During this time, consciously bring to mind a sense of warmth and compassion toward yourself and others. Visualize this compassion as a soothing light or energy, enveloping you and extending outward to people in your life.
- Whenever you encounter stressful situations or interactions throughout the day, pause and apply this mindful compassion. Ask yourself, "How can I respond with kindness?" This practice helps reinforce a compassionate outlook as a default response to life's challenges.

By engaging in these exercises, you are not only practicing forgiveness but are actively cultivating an inner landscape where compassion is abundant and self-healing is profound. These actions are steps toward liberating yourself from past hurts and embracing a future filled with emotional freedom and deeper connections.

Heartfelt Reflections: A Journey Within

These prompts are designed to be revisited. As you continue to grow and evolve, your responses might change, reflecting deeper insights and understanding. By regularly engaging with these reflections, you create a documented journey of your emotional evolution, which can be incredibly insightful and affirming as you navigate the complexities of forgiveness and self-compassion in your growth journey.

Journal Prompt 1: Reflecting on Self-Forgiveness

Recall a time when you found it particularly hard to forgive yourself. Maybe it was a mistake you made that had significant consequences, or perhaps it was a series of minor errors you couldn't seem to get past. Reflect on your emotions during this time—was there guilt, shame, or frustration? How did these feelings manifest in your daily life?

Now, with a deeper understanding of forgiveness, think about what you would say to your inner child about this incident. How would you comfort them? What words of forgiveness would you offer? Write a dialogue or a letter to your inner child explaining the power of forgiveness and how they, too, deserve it. Make sure to express that everyone makes mistakes and that it's natural and essential for growth. Let your inner child know they are loved and accepted, exactly as they are, mistakes and all.

.

_____

_____

_____

_____

_____

_____

_____

_____

_____

_____

_____

_____

_____

_____

_____

_____

_____

_____

_____

_____

_____

_____

_____

_____

_____

_____

_____

_____

Journal Prompt 2: Forgiving Others to Liberate Yourself

Consider a current or past relationship where forgiveness needs to be applied. It could be a friend, family member, or colleague—someone whose actions have left a lasting imprint of hurt in your life. Describe the situation and articulate the feelings of resentment that have developed. How have these negative emotions influenced your behavior and emotional state? How have they filtered into other areas of your life?

Reflect on how letting go of this resentment could transform your life. Imagine a future where this burden of anger is no longer weighing on your heart. What would change for you emotionally? How might your relationships improve? Write about the positive outcomes that forgiveness could bring. Consider the peace and freedom of releasing these toxic ties and how embracing forgiveness could lead to a fuller, more joyful existence.

_____

_____

_____

_____

_____

_____

_____

_____

_____

_____

_____

_____

_____

_____

_____

_____

_____

_____

_____

_____

_____

_____

_____

_____

_____

_____

_____

Journal Prompt 3: Celebrating Moments of Self-Compassion

Think about a moment this week when you showed yourself compassion. It might have been a small act, like allowing yourself an extra hour of sleep, or a significant one, like standing up for your needs in a challenging situation. Describe this act of kindness toward yourself in detail. How did you feel before, during, and after this act?

Reflect on how this moment of compassion impacted the rest of your day. Did it change your mood, interactions with others, or perhaps your outlook on that day? Consider how treating yourself with kindness altered the narrative of your internal dialogue. Writing about this experience can reinforce the importance of self-compassion and highlight how these practices benefit your emotional health and enhance your interactions and relationships with others.

_____

_____

_____

_____

_____

_____

_____

_____

_____

_____

_____

_____

_____

_____

_____

_____

_____

_____

_____

Forgiveness is key to healing your inner child, but you must learn to nurture and keep the growth and healing progressing. We will explore just how you can continue to nurture and love your inner child in the upcoming chapter.

Chapter Six

NURTURING YOUR INNER CHILD

To truly heal your inner child, you must recognize and never lose sight of his or her presence within you. This presence signifies your ongoing need for tenderness, care, and protection.

—John Bradshaw

My journey with my inner child began during a particularly stressful period in my adult life when I found myself struggling with feelings of inadequacy and fear that seemed to have no immediate cause. It was during therapy that I first heard the term "inner child," and I was skeptical about how looking back at my childhood could help with my current issues. However, as I began to engage with this younger part of myself, I uncovered long-forgotten joy and pain. Memories of spending hours in nature, which had been a refuge from the chaos of a troubled home life, surfaced. I realized how much I had missed that connection with the earth and how little room I'd made for play and wonder in my adult life.

This realization was a turning point. I began to carve out time for activities that delighted my inner child. Simple actions like walking barefoot on grass, coloring, and watching sunsets brought profound peace and a sense of wholeness I hadn't felt in years. This exploration of childhood joys wasn't about escaping adult responsibilities but integrating my inner child's needs into my life to create a more balanced and joyful existence.

Understanding Your Inner Child

Understanding your inner child is a concept that bridges the realms of psychological theory and deep, personal introspection. It taps into the essence of who we were at the dawn of our consciousness and examines how those early experiences echo throughout our adult lives. This concept invites us to revisit our earliest chapters, not through the lens of nostalgia but with an intent to understand and heal.

At its core, the inner child is that part of your psyche that holds your earliest memories and experiences. It is the repository of your first joys, fears, initial triumphs, and traumas. As children, we view the world with wonder and vulnerability, our emotional responses raw and unfiltered. Our Experiences during these formative years set the groundwork for our emotional responses as adults.

Why is it crucial to engage with this part of ourselves? The reason is simple yet profound: Unresolved emotions and unmet needs from childhood can profoundly influence our adult behavior, often in ways we don't consciously realize. These influences can manifest in various aspects of life, from forming relationships to perceiving our worth. For example, someone who experienced abandonment as a child may struggle with attachment issues or possess an overwhelming fear of being left, which could complicate their relationships.

Reconnecting with and understanding your inner child can lead to significant breakthroughs in self-awareness. It allows an individual to identify the source of deep-seated fears, anxieties, or destructive behavior patterns that may hold them back from authentic living. For instance, the adult who never feels "good enough" despite numerous achievements might discover that this feeling stems from a childhood need for parental approval that was never satisfied. Recognizing this can shift the adult's perspective from self-criticism to self-compassion, understanding that these feelings are not reflections of their true capabilities but echoes of past inadequacies imposed by others.

Engaging with your inner child involves practices that many might find surprisingly simple yet incredibly impactful. It could be as straightforward as allowing yourself an afternoon to engage in play—through art, music, or simply being outdoors—which might have been a source of pure joy in childhood. It also involves more contemplative practices such as journaling or therapy sessions where guided reflection helps bring to light the needs and experiences of the inner child.

Moreover, nurturing your inner child is about creating an ongoing dialogue between your adult self and childhood self. This dialogue helps heal old wounds by providing the understanding, protection, and validation the inner child did not receive when needed. This healing process is not about rewriting the past but about altering the past's impact on your present and future.

Signs of a Neglected Inner Child

Identifying the signs of a neglected inner child is crucial for understanding and addressing deep-seated emotional wounds that may not be immediately apparent but significantly impact our daily lives and relationships. The neglected inner child manifests in various ways, often as enduring patterns of behavior and emotional responses that seem disproportionate or inexplicable in our adult lives. Chronic insecurity, poor self-esteem, and destructive relationships are among the most poignant indicators of this neglect, each stemming from unresolved needs and traumas experienced during childhood.

Chronic Insecurity

Chronic insecurity often originates from an environment where a child's emotional needs are consistently overlooked or dismissed. If a child grows up feeling that their feelings are unimportant or, worse, invalid, they learn to doubt their worth and perceptions. This doubt can evolve into a pervasive insecurity that extends into adulthood. Adults who experience this neglect might find themselves constantly seeking validation from others because they never internalized the belief that they are inherently valuable and capable. They may question their decisions incessantly and feel chronically unsure about their place in the world. This insecurity can manifest in professional settings where they might shy away from promotions or challenges, fearing exposure as a fraud—an embodiment of the so-called impostor syndrome.

Poor Self-Esteem

Similarly, poor self-esteem can be traced back to a childhood where the intrinsic value of the self was undermined or unacknowledged. Poor self-esteem could stem from critical or unresponsive caregivers, competitive sibling environments, or punitive educational settings where children are made to feel that their best efforts are never good enough. The internalization of these attitudes results in adults who carry a nagging sense of inadequacy, regardless of their achievements. They may engage in negative self-talk, a form of internal dialogue where every mistake is magnified and every success minimized. This constant self-criticism maintains and even deepens the entrenched belief that they are less deserving or less capable than others around them.

Destructive Relationships

Destructive relationships in adulthood can also significantly indicate a neglected inner child. Individuals who repeatedly find themselves in relationships that are emotionally harmful or unfulfilling may be unconsciously replicating the dynamics they experienced in childhood. For example, if someone grew up witnessing an abusive relationship between parents, they might subconsciously believe that such relationships are normal. They may inadvertently seek similar dynamics, thinking that volatile or dismissive behavior is a component of love. Alternatively, if their emotional needs were frequently ignored or if they were conditioned to appease a caregiver's unreasonable demands, they might find themselves perpetually involved with partners who are emotionally unavailable or overly demanding.

Addressing the Neglected Inner Child

Understanding where these issues stem from is the first step toward healing. For those grappling with chronic insecurity, recognizing the source of these feelings can begin to diminish their power. Therapy, mindfulness practices, and self-help strategies focused on building self-worth and autonomy can be invaluable.

Individuals struggling with poor self-esteem might benefit from therapeutic interventions that focus on re-framing self-perceptions and gradually building a more compassionate and appreciative view of themselves. Exercises like positive affirmations, journaling successes, and setting personal boundaries can reinforce a more positive self-image.

For those dealing with destructive relationship patterns, counseling can offer insights and tools for recognizing unhealthy dynamics and learning healthier ways of relating. Support groups and therapy focused on relationship patterns can also provide the guidance and support needed to break these cycles.

In all these cases, healing the neglected inner child involves an ongoing commitment to recognizing and nurturing one's deepest needs, fostering an environment where the inner child feels seen, heard, and valued. This process alleviates the symptoms of neglect and empowers individuals to lead more fulfilling and emotionally healthy lives.

Techniques to Nurture Your Inner Child

Nurturing the inner child is essential for anyone seeking to heal from past wounds and embrace a fuller, more vibrant life. This nurturing involves engaging in activities that connect us to the joyful, uninhibited essence of our childhood selves, fostering an environment where we can flourish without the constraints of adult apprehensions and skepticism. Let's explore several effective techniques that facilitate this connection and promote a healing dialogue with the inner child.

Creative Expression through Art, Music, or Dance

Creative activities such as art, music, and dance allow us to bypass the often restrictive realm of verbal communication and connect with our feelings directly and viscerally. These activities tap into the non-verbal parts of our brain, where many early memories and emotions reside. For instance, drawing or painting can be a form of visual storytelling where colors and shapes translate into expressions of complex emotional landscapes that words might not capture. Similarly, music can resonate with the deepest fibers of our being, evoking memories and emotions that might have been long forgotten. Dance, too, uses the body's language to explore and express feelings, helping to release pent-up emotions and reclaim the joy of spontaneous movement.

Engaging regularly in these creative activities can act as a powerful therapeutic tool, providing an outlet for emotions that the inner child has repressed. It's not about the end product but rather the process of creation that helps heal and liberate the inner child.

Playfulness to Rekindle Joy and Spontaneity

Playfulness is a gateway to rediscovering the joy and spontaneity of childhood. As adults, we often undervalue play as unproductive or trivial. However, play is crucial for emotional health, as it relieves stress and ignites creativity and innovation. Engaging in play can mean different things for different people—playing board games, engaging in sports, building models, or even playful interactions with pets. Whatever form it takes, play helps to lighten the burdens of adult responsibilities and reconnects us to the carefree nature of our inner child.

Incorporating play into daily life can be as simple as setting aside time for activities with no purpose other than enjoyment and relaxation. Playing and integrating playfulness not only honors the inner child's need for fun but also balances our often overly structured lives with spontaneity and light-heartedness.

Journaling with Your Inner Child

1. Set the Scene

Choose a quiet and comfortable space where you won't be disturbed. Make this a welcoming area that might appeal to your younger self—perhaps include items like soft blankets, a favorite childhood book, or a soothing music playlist.

2. Start with a Letter

Begin by writing a letter to your inner child. Address the child you were at an age when you felt vulnerable, neglected, or misunderstood. Start with a simple greeting and express your intention to provide the support they need.

Example:

"Dear Little [Your Name],

I want you to know that I'm here for you now. I understand things were really tough, and you felt alone, but I will make sure you feel loved and safe."

3. Express Understanding and Compassion

Acknowledge the feelings your inner child might have experienced during difficult times. Validate these feelings and offer the comfort that was missing.

Example:

"I know how scared you felt when you had to deal with [a specific event]. It wasn't fair for you to go through that alone. I'm truly sorry you felt so sad, and I love you so much."

4. Invite Your Inner Child to Respond

Encourage your inner child to express their needs or unresolved emotions. You might switch pens or use a different color to visually differentiate the "voice" of your inner child.

Example:

"What do you wish I knew about how you feel? Is there anything you need from me now?"

5. Close with Affirmation

End your journaling session by affirming your commitment to care for your inner child. Promise regular check-ins and continuous support.

Example:

"I promise to keep this conversation going. I'm here to protect and cherish you, always."

_____

_____

_____

_____

_____

_____

_____

_____

_____

_____

_____

Establishing a Routine of Self-Care That Honors the Inner Child's Needs

A routine of self-care is crucial for nurturing the inner child. Creating a self-care routine means creating daily and weekly habits that reflect an understanding of and a commitment to meeting your inner child's needs. Such routines might include regular periods of rest, walks in nature, favorite meals, or quiet time for reading and reflection. By consistently attending to these needs, you affirm to your inner child that they are worthy of care and attention, which can be incredibly healing.

Creating Safe Spaces: Practical Tips on Building Environments at Home and Work

Creating safe spaces in both your home and work environments is crucial for nurturing your inner child, allowing this aspect of yourself to feel recognized, valued, and secure. Below are more detailed ways of doing this:

At Home

Transforming your living space into a sanctuary for your inner child involves more than just aesthetic changes; it's about fostering an environment where you feel completely at ease and free to express your true self.

- **Designate a Comfort Corner:** Identify a corner of your home where you can retreat to feel safe and rejuvenated. Equip this space with items that soothe you—soft blankets, comforting pillows, a stack of your favorite books, or even a small indoor fountain for soothing sounds.

- **Incorporate Elements of Nature:** Adding elements like plants, flowers, or even a small sandbox can evoke a sense of peace and grounding. These elements can act as a bridge to the simplicity and wonder of nature, similar to childhood play outdoors.

- **Create an Expression Wall:** Dedicate a wall or a bulletin board to hang art, photos from happy memories, inspirational quotes, or anything else that sparks joy and creativity. This visual collage serves as a daily reminder of what matters most to you and can be particularly uplifting.

At Work

Even in a professional environment, where personal expression might be more constrained, minor modifications can significantly improve the feeling of safety and nurturing in your space.

- **Personalize Your Workspace:** Start by bringing in personal items that comfort or motivate you. You could bring family photos, a small plant, artwork by your favorite artists, or crafts made by your children. These items personalize your space and remind you of your life outside work pressures.

- **Organize for Tranquility:** An organized workspace can significantly reduce stress. Use pleasant organizational tools that not only serve a function but are also aesthetically pleasing. Choose colors and textures that calm you, and keep your space clutter-free to maintain a sense of order and tranquility.

- **Sensory Objects:** Keep a drawer or a small box with items that engage your senses and can provide a quick mental break or stress relief when needed. Sensory objects can include stress balls, scented candles or essential oils, tactile toys, or even a stash of your favorite treats.

By intentionally creating these safe spaces at home and work, you're not just designing areas conducive to relaxation and productivity; you're also actively honoring and responding to the needs of your inner child. These spaces symbolize your commitment to self-care and emotional well-being, reminding you daily that your needs matter and are worthy of attention.

In essence, each of these techniques validates and celebrates the inner child, helping to heal past traumas by fostering an environment where the inner child feels seen, heard, and cherished. As you incorporate these practices into your life, you may find that you not only heal old wounds but also rediscover a sense of wonder, joy, and spontaneity that enriches every aspect of your existence.

Exercises for Regular Inner Child Nurturing

Connecting with your inner child is essential to nurturing your overall emotional health. It helps rediscover the unfiltered joy and enthusiasm we often experience in childhood, bringing a refreshing perspective to the often mundane routines of adult life. Here are two thoughtfully designed exercises that are not just simple but deeply effective in rekindling the spirit of your inner child, helping you to integrate playfulness and joy into your daily life.

Exercise 1: Create a Joy List
The first exercise involves creating what we'll call a "joy list." This list should include activities that brought you immense happiness as a child. Think back to those carefree days—what were you doing? Were you splashing around in a puddle, crafting little art projects, flying kites on windy days, or perhaps getting lost in the pages of fairy tales?

Begin by jotting down all these activities. Don't worry about how silly or trivial they might seem now; the key is to reconnect with those genuine moments of happiness. Your list might include things like riding bicycles, building forts, painting, dancing freely to your favorite tunes, or chasing fireflies as dusk falls.

Once you have your list, incorporate at least one of these activities into your weekly routine. This integration bridges your current self and your inner child, affirming that joy is a vital part of your life, not just a distant memory. For instance, if you loved to draw as a child, carry a small sketchbook and doodle in your free moments. If you enjoyed dancing, start or end your day with a song that uplifts your spirit and move to the rhythm without any inhibitions.

Exercise 2: Spend an Afternoon Being Childlike

The second exercise is about immersing yourself in an afternoon of childlike play, which can be incredibly liberating and a fun way to disconnect from the pressures of adult responsibilities. Choose an activity that resonates with your inner child's desires—perhaps something from your "joy list" or a new idea that strikes you as exciting.

You might visit a local playground. Swing on the swings, slide down the slides, or find a sandbox and build a sandcastle. If a playground doesn't feel right, you could stay indoors and color, getting yourself an adult coloring book or a children's version with characters you loved. Alternatively, watching your favorite childhood movies can be a powerful way to connect with your inner child. Make it special by creating a cozy fort with blankets and pillows in your living room, with a bowl of popcorn and a sense of adventure.

As you engage in these activities, pay attention to how you feel. It's normal to feel silly or self-conscious at first but allow yourself to embrace the experience fully. Notice if there's a sense of liberation, happiness, or perhaps emotional release. These activities are not about reverting to childhood permanently but about allowing the uninhibited part of your personality to come out and play, reminding you that life is not just about responsibilities and routines.

Heartfelt Reflections: A Journey Within

When we suppress emotions as children, we often do so because our environments may not have felt safe enough to express sadness, fear, or anger. These emotions don't vanish; instead, they hide beneath the surface, sometimes emerging as anxiety, depression, or unexplained irritability in our adult lives. To truly heal, we must create a safe space within ourselves to confront these hidden feelings, acknowledge their sources, and understand their impact on our current behavior.

Journal Prompt 1: Identifying Suppressed Emotions

- Reflect on moments from your childhood when you felt you had to hide your emotions. What were these emotions? Write about these instances and try to describe how you felt.
- How might these moments have influenced the way you handle emotions now? Are there emotions you still find difficult to express?

_____

_____

_____

_____

_____

_____

_____

_____

_____

_____

_____

_____

_____

_____

Journal Prompt 2: Dialogue with Your Inner Child

- Imagine a conversation with your younger self who experienced these emotions. What would you say to comfort them? How would you validate their feelings that were once ignored or suppressed?
- Write what your inner child might say in return. What emotions are they still holding on to? What do they need from you now?

_____

_____

_____

_____

_____

_____

_____

_____

_____

_____

_____

_____

_____

Journal Prompt 3: Envisioning Release and Relief

- Visualize a scenario where you allow yourself to fully feel and express these suppressed emotions safely. What does this look like? How does it feel to let these emotions surface finally?

- Describe the sense of relief or other feelings that come from acknowledging these parts of your inner child. What changes might occur in your life if you were able to regularly acknowledge and work through these emotions?

_____

_____

_____

_____

_____

_____

_____

_____

_____

_____

_____

_____

_____

_____

_____

_____

_____

These prompts are designed to facilitate a deep and compassionate exploration of your inner child's suppressed emotions. By courageously facing these parts of yourself, you're not only acknowledging your inner child's experiences but also actively engaging in the healing process. This journey of reflection can lead to profound personal growth and a more integrated sense of self.

Your inner child has likely developed some bad habits of negative self-talk. Let's jump right in and explore how you can transform your inner monologue into one of self-compassion.

Chapter Seven

TRANSFORMING NEGATIVE SELF-TALK INTO SELF-COMPASSION

❧

> **❝** *Talk to yourself like you would to someone you love.* **❞**
>
> —*Brené Brown*

How often do we find ourselves trapped in the clutches of our harsh criticism? It's a common experience where the voice inside us that should be our ally turns into our harshest critic. This internal dialogue, if left unchecked, can significantly erode our self-esteem and distort the lens through which we view ourselves and our capabilities. This chapter delves into understanding this critical inner voice and transforming it into a compassionate dialogue that nurtures and profoundly supports our inner child.

The roots of this critical inner voice often trace back to our early experiences. As children, we absorb the attitudes and responses of the adults around us, forming the foundation of our self-perception. If the feedback from significant caregivers was overly critical or we were exposed to constant comparison and high expectations, we might have internalized a voice that echoes these sentiments—one that rarely gives us credit and frequently points out our flaws.

Addressing this requires us to first recognize the patterns of this negative self-talk. Are we continually berating ourselves for perceived failures? Do we downplay our achievements? Understanding these patterns is the first step toward transforming them. It involves shifting our internal dialogue from criticism to compassion, from dismissal to validation. This transformation is not about silencing the inner critic; it's about reshaping its messages to encourage growth and self-acceptance.

Understanding Negative Self-Talk

Understanding negative self-talk involves delving into the origins of the critical inner voices that often haunt our adult lives. These voices, echoing through our thoughts, are not mere remnants of past conversations but are deeply entwined with our earliest experiences. In childhood, the foundation of how we perceive ourselves and how we think others perceive us is laid down, often dictating the tone and content of our self-dialogue as adults.

For many, the seeds of negative self-talk are sown in an environment where criticism overshadows encouragement. If, as children, we were frequently corrected in harsh or dismissive ways, we might have internalized the belief that we are inherently flawed or inadequate. A child receiving more feedback about what they are doing wrong than what they are doing right may grow to view themselves through a lens of perpetual deficiency. This critical perspective can persist as a nagging voice in their head that replays old, painful echoes of disapproval.

Additionally, negative self-talk can stem from an environment where high expectations are the norm. In families or schools where excellence is expected and only extraordinary achievements are celebrated, children may feel that ordinary successes are unworthy. This setting can cultivate a mindset where one's best efforts are never quite good enough, fostering feelings of inadequacy that spill over into adult self-perception.

Children are also adept at picking up and internalizing the unspoken attitudes of their caregivers. Subtle cues, such as a parent's disapproving sigh or a teacher's skeptical look, can be as impactful as direct criticism. These cues can subtly inform a child that they are disappointing or not living up to expectations, even if the words are never spoken. As these children grow, the critical voices echo, filling the gaps between their accomplishments with doubt and self-criticism.

Moreover, if a child grows up feeling different—whether due to appearance, abilities, or interests—and these differences are not celebrated or are marginalized, they might internalize feelings of alienation or inferiority. These types of emotions and experiences too can evolve into a critical inner voice that questions their worth and right to belong.

To combat negative self-talk, it's crucial to recognize its roots in these early life experiences. Awareness is the first step toward transformation. By understanding that these internalized voices are not truths but echoes of past interactions, we can begin to challenge and reshape them. Techniques like cognitive-behavioral therapy (CBT), mindfulness practices, and positive affirmations can be effective tools in rewriting the narratives that fuel negative self-talk.

The Impact of Self-Criticism

Persistent negative self-talk is not just harmful banter; it's a deep-seated pattern that significantly impacts our mental and emotional health, directly affecting our inner child—the most genuine version of ourselves from our earliest years.

Psychological and Emotional Impact

Negative self-talk distorts our self-image and diminishes our self-esteem, leading to stress, anxiety, and depression. This relentless internal criticism puts the body in a constant state of stress, causing emotional and physical exhaustion. Over time, this can inhibit personal growth by fostering a mindset that avoids new challenges and opportunities, trapping us in a cycle of self-doubt and missed experiences.

The damage extends to our inner child, exacerbating old wounds and blocking the healing process. Each negative thought not only reinforces adult insecurities but also reopens past emotional wounds from childhood. These negative thoughts prevent the inner child from healing, affecting our emotional resilience and the ability to form healthy relationships.

Transforming Self-Criticism into Self-Compassion

To heal our present and past selves, we must shift from self-criticism to self-compassion. This transformation involves:

- **Awareness:** Recognizing patterns of negative self-talk.
- **Replacement:** Challenging and replacing harmful narratives with kinder, truthful assessments.
- **Mindfulness:** Using mindfulness to detach from and observe negative thoughts non-judgmentally.
- **Therapy:** Engaging in therapeutic approaches like Cognitive Behavioral Therapy (CBT) and specific therapies to heal the inner child, such as Inner Child Therapy or EMDR.

By cultivating a compassionate inner dialogue, we not only improve our mental health but also allow our inner child to heal and thrive. This shift enables us to engage more fully with life, embracing our experiences with greater confidence and joy.

Building a Compassionate Inner Voice

Cultivating self-compassion is essential in the journey of personal growth. It's about transforming the often harsh dialogue we have with ourselves into one that is nurturing and supportive. By fostering a compassionate inner voice, we enhance our emotional well-being and empower ourselves to face life's challenges with resilience and grace. Here are practical strategies for cultivating self-compassion and concrete steps for building and reinforcing a compassionate inner voice daily.

Strategies for Cultivating Self-Compassion and a Compassionate Inner Voice

- **Reframing Techniques:** Reframing involves changing your perspective on a challenging situation to view it in a more positive or realistic light. It helps shift your internal narrative from one of criticism or victimhood to one of empowerment and understanding. For instance, instead of thinking, "I failed that project, and I'm incompetent," you could reframe it to, "The project didn't go as planned, but I learned valuable lessons that will help me improve next time."

- **Regular Practice:** Like any skill, developing a compassionate inner voice requires regular practice. Set aside time each day for activities that encourage self-compassion. Regular practice could be a few minutes of morning meditation, writing in a gratitude journal, or engaging in self-care practices that make you feel nurtured and respected.

- **Self-Compassion Breaks:** Whenever you find yourself slipping into self-criticism, take a "self-compassion break." A break involves stopping what you're doing to offer yourself kindness and understanding. Place a hand over your heart, breathe deeply, and speak or think gently to yourself, just as you would to a dear friend in distress.

- **Educate Yourself:** Learning more about self-compassion can reinforce its importance and give you a more extraordinary toolkit of strategies. Reading books, listening to podcasts, or even attending workshops on self-compassion can provide ongoing support and inspiration.

- **Reflective Writing:** Regularly write down your thoughts and feelings. Reflective writing can help you become more aware of your inner dialogue's tone and make adjustments toward more compassionate self-talk. Reflect on situations where you were hard on yourself and write a more empathetic response.

Exercises for Implementation

In this chapter's challenge, we engage in an exercise designed to shift the dynamics of our inner dialogue from self-criticism to self-compassion. By identifying and transforming the negative statements we begin to nurture a more supportive relationship with our inner selves.

Exercise: Transforming Negative Self-Talk

Step 1: Identify Negative Statements

Begin by reflecting on your thoughts in recent days or during specific challenging situations. Identify three common negative statements that frequently surface in your mind. These might be thoughts like "I'm not smart enough to figure this out," "I always mess things up," or "No one cares about what I have to say." Write these down.

Step 2: Craft Compassionate Responses

Next to each negative statement, write a compassionate response. This response should counter the negativity, providing support and understanding to yourself as you would offer to a good friend. For example:

- For "I'm not smart enough to figure this out," you might write, "I am capable of learning and growing, and it's okay to ask for help when I need it."
- Replace "I always mess things up" with "Everyone makes mistakes, and each error is a step toward growth. I am learning, and that's what truly matters."
- Instead of "No one cares about what I have to say," try "My thoughts and feelings are valid and deserve to be heard. I will express myself and find those who appreciate my contributions."

Step 3: Reflect on the Shift

After you have written your compassionate responses, take a moment to reflect on how the tone of dialogue changes. How does it feel to address yourself with kindness rather than criticism? Observe any shifts in your emotional state or how you perceive the challenge at hand.

This exercise is not just about creating a momentary feel-good factor; it's a fundamental shift in how we relate to ourselves. Over time, practicing this method can significantly alter our self-perception, leading to greater confidence and emotional resilience. Engage with this exercise regularly to deepen your practice of self-compassion and transform your internal narrative.

Heartfelt Reflections: A Journey Within

Engaging with your inner world through reflective journaling can be a transformative experience. It allows you to explore the depths of your emotions and the narratives you tell yourself. This exercise helps cultivate a more compassionate self-dialogue, guiding you to replace self-criticism with understanding and support.

Journal Prompt 1: Reflect on Self-Criticism

Think about a recent instance where you were particularly hard on yourself. Maybe you missed a deadline, said something awkward, or just had a bad day. Reflect on what you told yourself during this time. Now, consider if a friend were in the same situation. What would you say to them? Write down the compassionate words you would offer to a friend, and notice how they differ from the words you directed at yourself.

_____

_____

_____

_____

_____

_____

_____

_____

_____

_____

_____

Journal Prompt 2: The Impact of Compassionate Self-Talk

Reflect on an occasion when you consciously shifted your internal monologue from harsh or negative to supportive and compassionate. Describe the situation and the negative self-talk you experienced. Then, write about how you changed that dialogue to something more positive. How did this shift affect your emotions throughout the day? Did you notice any changes in how you felt physically or emotionally as a result?

_____

_____

_____

_____

_____

_____

_____

_____

_____

_____

_____

_____

_____

_____

_____

Journal Prompt 3: Dialogue with Your Inner Child

Imagine a scenario where you can speak directly to your inner child—the version of you that still holds onto past hurts and fears. Think about a specific instance from childhood when you felt criticized or unsupported. What does your inner child need to hear at that moment? Write a dialogue between your adult self and your inner child, offering the support, understanding, and encouragement needed then. What comforting words would you share? How would you reassure your younger self?

_____

_____

_____

_____

_____

_____

_____

_____

_____

_____

_____

_____

_____

_____

_____

These prompts are designed to deepen your connection with yourself, encouraging a shift toward self-compassion that nurtures both your adult self and inner child. By regularly practicing this reflective writing, you can develop a kinder inner voice that supports your overall well-being and fosters a healthier, more loving relationship with yourself.

Your inner child is dying to express themselves, and they have all this pent up energy that needs to be released. It's time to learn how to heal your wounded inner child through the art of self-expression!

Chapter Eight

Chapter Eight
HEALING THROUGH SELF-EXPRESSION

> *Art opens the closets, airs out the cellars and attics. It brings healing.*
> —Julia Cameron

The healing power of self-expression in nurturing the inner child is profound and vital. Creative processes offer more than just an outlet for artistic exploration; they provide a unique pathway to access and heal the deep-seated wounds of our younger selves. Through activities like painting, writing, music, and dance, we can communicate complex emotions that might be difficult to articulate through words alone, fostering a sense of release and understanding essential for emotional recovery.

Why does self-expression have such a potent effect on our inner child? At its core, the inner child represents our most primal form of self, embodying our earliest joyful and painful experiences. This part of us often holds onto past traumas and negative experiences that were never fully processed or understood. Creative expression allows us to revisit these emotions in a safe and controlled environment, turning intangible feelings and memories into tangible artwork, stories, music, or dance movements. This transformation is not just symbolic; it enables us to externalize our feelings, examine them, and reframe them in ways that promote healing.

For instance, drawing or painting can be particularly effective for visual thinkers. Choosing colors and forms that resonate with specific emotions can help a person visualize their feelings, making them more manageable and less overwhelming. Similarly, writing can be a powerful tool for those who feel comforted by the structure of words. Composing poems or stories about personal experiences allows individuals to narrate their healing journey, providing perspective and catharsis.

Music and dance connect with the inner child on a primal level, often reaching parts of the psyche that other forms of communication cannot. Music's rhythm and melodies can evoke deep emotional responses, offering a healing resonance with the body's rhythms. At the same time, dance utilizes physical movement to express and release emotions, helping to heal and integrate both body and mind.

How does engaging in these creative processes specifically help heal the inner child? By providing a voice to the unspoken, these activities validate the experiences and emotions of the inner child. They reassure this vulnerable part of ourselves that it is heard, understood, and valued. Moreover, creating something new—a piece of art, a set of lyrics, a dance routine—can be incredibly empowering. It shifts the individual from a state of passivity, where things happen to them, to one of agency, where they are the creators of their narrative.

Incorporating self-expression into regular practice can be transformative. It strengthens the communication between the adult self and the inner child, reinforcing a bond essential for integrated healing. This ongoing dialogue ensures that the inner child is not just a shadow of the past but a living, active part of the individual's present emotional life, contributing to a richer, more fulfilled existence.

Ultimately, the power of self-expression lies in its ability to transcend ordinary communication, touching the depths of the human spirit where profound healing can occur. It is a testament to the resilience of the human heart and its capacity for recovery and joy, no matter the wounds it carries.

Different Ideas for Self-Expression

Embracing various modes of self-expression can profoundly enrich our emotional lives, providing relief and release and a deeper understanding of our inner landscapes. Art therapy, writing, music and dance, and drama therapy are all powerful tools for articulating what often lies buried beneath the surface—our deepest fears, joys, and memories. Integrating these expressive activities into daily life is not just therapeutic; it's a path to sustained emotional health and a vibrant, fulfilling existence.

Art Therapy

Art therapy involves using painting, drawing, or sculpting to navigate and process emotions. This form of expression allows you to externalize what you feel, giving form to emotions that can be hard to articulate. To integrate art therapy into daily life, start with small, manageable projects. Keep a sketchbook where you doodle, paint, or draw for a few minutes each day. Use colors and shapes that resonate with your mood, allowing your subconscious to guide your choices.

Writing

Writing, whether it's journaling, poetry, or storytelling, serves as a powerful catharsis. It can help clarify thoughts and feelings, providing a safe space for introspection and self-analysis. To make writing a part of your everyday routine, start a daily journal. Each night, spend some time reflecting on your day, expressing not just events but how they made you feel. Alternatively, try composing a short poem now and then, focusing on specific emotional experiences or general reflections on your life.

Music and Dance

Expressing feelings through music creation, singing, or dance can be incredibly liberating. These activities connect with the primal parts of our brain, stimulating emotional release and joy. Incorporate music and dance into your daily life by setting aside time each week to play an instrument, sing, or dance in your living room. Create playlists that resonate with different moods and allow yourself spontaneous moments to dance or sing along, fully experiencing the emotional spectrum music evokes.

Drama Therapy

Drama therapy involves role-playing to explore personal interactions and past experiences. Drama therapy can be particularly effective in understanding different perspectives and processing past events. To practice drama therapy at home, engage in imaginative role-play that reflects recent interactions or longstanding personal challenges. Sometimes, acting out these scenarios in the privacy of your home can lead to new insights and emotional release.

Practical Tips for Daily Integration

- **Set Realistic Goals:** Start small and gradually increase the complexity of your activities as they become a more routine part of your life.
- **Create a Dedicated Space:** If possible, dedicate a specific area in your home for your creative activities. Your dedicated space can be a writing desk, an art corner, or a comfortable chair where you sit with your journal.
- **Schedule Time:** Just as you would schedule a meeting or a doctor's appointment, schedule time for your expressive activities. Making them a fixed part of your day ensures consistency.
- **Combine Activities:** Don't feel limited to one form of expression. Combine them as you see fit—dance while listening to music, sketch in your journal, or write a poem after a role-playing session.

Integrating these forms of self-expression into your daily life helps maintain emotional health. It also builds a deeper connection with your inner self, fostering growth, healing, and a profound sense of joy.

Healing Exercises

Engaging in creative exercises can be an extremely beneficial method to reconnect with the often-neglected inner child within us all. Each artistic endeavor allows us to explore and express the emotions tied to our earliest, most formative experiences, providing insights and healing.

Exercise 1: Create a Piece of Art

Choose a significant childhood memory, perhaps a moment of joy, sadness, or a turning point in your early life. Use your preferred medium—whether it's paint, charcoal, clay, or crayons to create a piece of art that captures the essence of this memory. As you work, focus on the emotions that arise. Notice how your hands move, how the colors blend, and how the image takes shape. This process isn't just about the final artwork; it's about allowing yourself to feel and perhaps understand these emotions more intensely.

Exercise 2: Write a Poem

Sit quietly for a moment and reconnect with your inner child. Think about what they felt, feared, or dreamed of. Now, write a poem from the perspective of your inner child, giving voice to their experiences and feelings. This exercise isn't about crafting the perfect verse but rather about letting your inner child speak through you, using rhythm and rhyme to add depth and emotion to their words.

Exercise 3: Dance to Your Favorite Music

Listen to music that holds special significance, perhaps something you loved in childhood or a tune that brings back memories. Let yourself dance freely to this music, not choreographed or restrained, but simply moving in any way you feel compelled. Pay attention to any emotions that surface as you move. Dancing allows your body to speak when words might fail, providing a powerful release for feelings you might not even have known were there.

Heartfelt Reflections: A Journey Within

Embarking on a journey of creative self-expression opens up pathways to the deeper parts of our psyche, allowing us to explore and connect with our long-neglected inner child. These journal prompts are designed to deepen your reflection on the exercises of creating art, writing poetry, and dancing freely. They aim to guide you through an deliberative process that uncovers hidden emotions and enhances your understanding of how these formative feelings continue to shape your adult life.

Journal Prompt 1: Reflections on Creating Art

After completing your art piece that represents a significant childhood memory, take a moment to reflect on the creative process and the outcome. How did you feel while creating your artwork? Were there any unexpected emotions or memories that surfaced during this activity? Write about the sensations, thoughts, and emotions you experienced. This act can help you understand the impact of visual and artistic expression and its power to unlock hidden aspects of your past.

_____

_____

_____

_____

_____

_____

_____

_____

_____

_____

_____

_____

Journal Prompt 2: Experiencing Free Dance

Describe your experience during your free dance session. Focus on how your body felt as you moved without constraints. What emotions came to the forefront during this expressive exercise? Did the movement help you release or better understand these emotions? Writing about this bodily form of expression can illuminate how physical movement and dance are powerful tools for emotional release and self-expression.

_____

_____

_____

_____

_____

_____

_____

_____

_____

_____

_____

_____

_____

_____

_____

_____

By engaging with these journal prompts, you invite a deeper connection with yourself, offering a unique opportunity to reconcile with your inner child. Let's continue this journey and dive into the intricacies of nurturing kindness, and how this can help heal your wounds.

Chapter Nine

NURTURING KINDNESS

> *Be kind to yourself as you proceed along this journey. This kindness, in itself, is a means of awakening the spark of love within you and helping others to discover that spark within themselves.*
>
> —Tsoknyi Rinpoche

Understanding self-kindness is crucial in a world that often prioritizes achievement, productivity, and relentless self-improvement. Self-kindness involves treating oneself with the same care, compassion, and understanding that we would offer to a good friend. It's about recognizing our worthiness of love and care, even when we fail or make mistakes. This gentle and accepting approach to ourselves is foundational for building resilience, maintaining emotional well-being, and cultivating a fulfilling life.

Why does self-kindness matter? At its core, self-kindness influences how we navigate life's challenges and relationships with others. When we are kind to ourselves, we acknowledge that being imperfect, failing, and experiencing difficulties are all part of the human experience. This acknowledgment allows us to approach setbacks with a mindset that views these experiences as opportunities for growth rather than as indictments of our value or capabilities.

Practicing self-kindness also profoundly affects our mental health. It reduces the impact of stress, wards off feelings of depression and anxiety, and fosters greater life satisfaction. These effects happen because self-kindness directly counters the often automatic habit of self-criticism—a pattern that can lead to significant psychological distress.

Moreover, when we're compassionate with ourselves, we're more likely to recover from mistakes more quickly and to persist in the face of challenges. This resilience enhances our lives and equips us to be more empathetic and supportive in our interactions. Being kind to ourselves teaches us how to genuinely extend kindness to the world, enhancing our relationships and communities.

Techniques and Exercises for Nurturing Self-Kindness

In our journey toward self-compassion, various techniques can enrich and deepen our understanding of kindness toward ourselves. From visualization and personal rituals to leveraging technology and nature, these methods provide a diverse toolkit for nurturing a compassionate self-view.

Visualization Techniques

Visualization, or guided imagery, is a powerful psychological tool that can transform our internal dialogue. By imagining ourselves in scenarios where we are treated with kindness and compassion, we can begin to shift our self-perception. For instance, picture yourself surrounded by a warm, gentle light that soothes and heals self-doubt or criticism. This light represents unconditional love and acceptance. Regular practice of this visualization can help solidify feelings of self-worth and kindness.

Personal Rituals

Establishing personal rituals is another effective way to cultivate self-kindness. These rituals can be simple, such as starting the day by stating a positive affirmation in the mirror or taking a few minutes each evening to write down three things you appreciated about yourself that day. These acts, though minor, reinforce a positive and nurturing relationship with oneself and can become anchors of self-compassion in daily life.

Using Technology for Kindness

In our digital age, technology can also support our self-kindness journey. Numerous apps are designed to promote mindfulness, deliver daily affirmations, or guide users through meditation sessions focused on compassion. By integrating these tools into our routines, we can access reminders and prompts that encourage a kinder self-dialogue.

The Role of Nature in Self-Kindness

Connecting with nature is inherently soothing and restorative. Walking through a park or sitting by a river can provide a serene backdrop for introspection and self-kindness. Nature reminds us of the natural rhythms of life, encouraging us to treat ourselves with the gentle ebb and flow of compassion we observe in the world around us.

Practical Exercises to Enhance Self-Kindness

Exercise 1: Create a personal kindness mantra. Develop a mantra that embodies compassion and understanding toward yourself. Repeat this mantra daily to reinforce positive self-regard and internal support.

Exercise 2: Engage in a "kindness walk." Choose a natural setting for a walk where you intentionally focus on self-compassion thoughts. Each step can be a physical manifestation of kindness toward yourself, perhaps reflecting on your mantra or noticing the beauty around you as a mirror of your inner beauty.

Through these varied approaches—visualization, personal rituals, technology, and nature—we can build a multifaceted practice of self-kindness that not only supports our emotional and mental health but also enhances our ability to extend kindness to others. Each technique reinforces the fundamental truth that being kind to ourselves is a necessary step in experiencing a complete, balanced, and connected life.

Heartfelt Reflections: A Journey Within

These journal prompts are designed to help you explore the nuances of your experiences with self-kindness, and cultivate a deeper, more compassionate connection with yourself.

Journal Prompt 1: Reflection on a Personal Mantra

Reflect on the process of creating a personal mantra. How did it feel to articulate a phrase that encapsulates kindness toward yourself? Consider any shifts in your internal dialogue since introducing this mantra. Has repeating these words begun to change the way you talk to yourself throughout the day? Write about the emotional responses or changes in self-perception that this mantra may have ignited.

_____

_____

_____

_____

_____

_____

_____

_____

_____

_____

_____

_____

_____

_____

_____

_____

_____

_____

_____

_____

_____

Journal Prompt 2: Insights from Your Kindness Walk

Describe your experiences during your kindness walk. As you walked, what thoughts surfaced? Focus on the feelings that arose as you intentionally treated yourself compassionately and observed the natural environment. What insights did you gain about how to treat yourself with more kindness? Did walking in nature influence your ability to extend compassion to yourself?

_____

_____

_____

_____

_____

_____

_____

_____

_____

_____

_____

_____

_____

_____

_____

_____

_____

_____

_____

_____

_____

_____

_____

_____

These reflections offer valuable windows into your evolving relationship with yourself, highlighting the power of intentional practices in nurturing self-compassion.

In the journey of healing your inner child, setting firm boundaries emerges as a vital step toward cultivating tranquility and self-respect. The upcoming chapter explores how establishing clear limits can create a safe space for your inner child to heal and thrive, allowing you to embrace a peaceful and empowered existence.

Chapter Ten

SETTING BOUNDARIES AND FINDING PEACE

> *Daring to set boundaries is about having the courage to love ourselves even when we risk disappointing others.*
>
> —Brené Brown

U nderstanding and setting boundaries is akin to drawing a personal map that outlines the territories where we allow others to enter and where we need to stand alone. These boundaries are essential in protecting our inner child—the core of our emotional and psychological well-being. Setting boundaries is not about building walls but defining our limits clearly and compassionately, ensuring we respect ourselves and teach others to do the same. This self-respect is fundamental to healing, as it prevents old wounds from reopening and provides the inner child with a sense of security and worth.

Boundaries come in various forms, each serving a distinct purpose in safeguarding our well-being.

- **Emotional Boundaries** involve protecting yourself from being overly responsible for someone else's emotions or letting others dictate how you feel. These boundaries allow you to feel your emotions without apology and protect your right to your emotional experiences without being overwhelmed by other's feelings.

- **Physical Boundaries** pertain to your personal space and physical touch. They help you determine who can touch you, how, and under what circumstances, ensuring your comfort and safety.

- **Intellectual Boundaries** relate to your thoughts, ideas, and beliefs. Setting these boundaries means respecting your opinions and not allowing others to belittle your thoughts or force their ideologies onto you.

- **Spiritual Boundaries** protect your right to your belief system and spiritual practices. They involve respecting your values and rituals and not allowing others to impose their spiritual beliefs on you.

Each type of boundary you set is a guardian for your inner child, shielding you from potential emotional, physical, intellectual, or spiritual intrusions that could trigger past traumas. By clearly defining and communicating these limits, you protect your inner child and nurture an environment where they can thrive. This process empowers you to heal, grow, and move forward with confidence and peace.

Recognizing Boundary Violations

Recognizing when our boundaries are violated is crucial for maintaining mental and emotional health. Often, we may not even realize that a boundary has been crossed until we feel the aftermath—a tangle of negative emotions that can leave us feeling unsettled, disrespected, or overwhelmed. Understanding these emotional signals and recognizing the signs of boundary violations can empower us to take action and reassert our needs.

A primary indicator of a boundary violation is the feeling of discomfort. This discomfort might initially be subtle, a quiet unease you can't quite pinpoint. It's a signal from your inner self that something isn't right. Pay attention to this feeling. Does interacting with a particular person always leave you feeling drained or upset? Do certain environments make you anxious? These are clues that your limits are being challenged.

Resentment is another powerful sign that your boundaries may be compromised. It often arises when we feel taken advantage of or say yes to something against our better judgment. Resentment can fester, leading to a buildup of anger and frustration. It's a sign that we need to reevaluate our boundaries and assert them more clearly to prevent future breaches.

Feeling overwhelmed is also a common response to boundary violations. This overwhelm can occur when too much is being asked of us, whether emotionally, physically, or intellectually, and we haven't set a firm limit. Overwhelm can manifest as anxiety, exhaustion, or a sense of being lost to the demands of others. It's your psyche's way of signaling that it's time to step back and reassess your boundaries.

Identifying these emotional responses and understanding their origins is the first step in protecting your boundaries. When you notice these feelings, take a moment to reflect: What boundary might have been crossed? Who was involved? Understanding the context can help you clarify your boundaries and develop strategies to assert them, ensuring your emotional and psychological space is respected and preserved.

Steps to Setting Healthy Boundaries

Setting healthy boundaries is an essential act of self-care that protects your emotional energy and fosters genuine relationships. Here's a concise guide on establishing and maintaining these boundaries effectively.

Step 1: Identify Your Limits

Start by understanding what you can tolerate and accept in different interactions. Reflect on past experiences that made you uncomfortable and use these insights to define your limits clearly.

Step 2: Communicate Your Boundaries Clearly

Once you know your limits, communicate them clearly and assertively to others. Use "I" statements to express your needs respectfully, such as "I feel overwhelmed when I take on extra tasks at work. I need to focus on my assigned projects."

Step 3: Prepare for Pushback

When you first set boundaries, expect some pushback. People might test your limits or react negatively. Stay firm and reiterate your boundaries calmly. Explain the importance of these limits for your well-being.

Step 4: Reinforce Your Boundaries

It is crucial to consistently reinforce your boundaries. If someone repeatedly disrespects your boundaries, consider reducing your availability or discussing the issue further to emphasize your needs.

Step 5: Self-Reflect and Adjust

Finally, regularly reflect on and adjust your boundaries as needed. As your circumstances and relationships evolve, so too might your needs and limits.

Following these steps, you can set boundaries that honor your values and emotional health, creating a more balanced and fulfilling life.

Boundaries with Self

Setting boundaries isn't just about managing how others treat us—it's also crucial to set boundaries with ourselves. This internal discipline is essential for maintaining mental health and overall well-being. It involves recognizing our limits and committing not to push beyond them, thereby respecting our needs as diligently as we respect the needs of others.

Self-boundaries might include limiting self-criticism, a common habit that can spiral into negative self-talk and diminished self-esteem. Setting a boundary here means consciously stopping those critical thoughts and replacing them with more compassionate and supportive messages. For instance, instead of telling yourself, "I'm so inefficient," you could say, "I'm working at my own pace, and that's okay."

Another important self-boundary is knowing when to take breaks. In our high-speed, always-connected world, it's easy to push through fatigue, ignoring signs of burnout. Setting firm boundaries about work hours or daily relaxation time helps preserve energy and prevent burnout. Setting this kind of boundary could look like committing to not checking emails after a particular hour, ensuring leisure activities are part of your weekly schedule, or simply allowing yourself time to unwind each evening without guilt.

By setting and respecting these personal boundaries, you not only safeguard your well-being but also enhance your capacity to manage external relationships with greater clarity and calm.

Healthy Exercises

In this chapter's challenge, we delve into practical exercises designed to strengthen your ability to set and maintain boundaries. These activities will help you identify, articulate, and affirm your boundaries, enhancing your confidence and protecting your inner well-being.

Exercise 1: Identify Your Boundary Needs

Start by reflecting on your life to pinpoint areas where your boundaries might be weak or missing. Consider various aspects such as work, relationships, and personal time. Write down situations where you feel drained, uncomfortable, or overextended. Next, think about what changes you could implement to strengthen these boundaries. These changes could involve saying no to additional responsibilities, asking for privacy, or simply giving yourself permission to disconnect.

Exercise 2: Role-Playing Boundary Setting

Role-playing is a powerful tool to practice boundary-setting in a safe environment. You can do this alone in front of a mirror or with a trusted friend. Create scenarios that typically challenge your boundaries. Practice clear and assertive communication in these roles. For example, rehearse how to decline extra work from a colleague or request personal space from a family member. This exercise will help build your confidence in maintaining boundaries in real situations.

Exercise 3: Create a Boundary Affirmation

Develop personal affirmations that reinforce the importance and legitimacy of your boundaries. These could be statements like "I have the right to protect my time and energy" or "I am worthy of respect and understanding from myself and others." Write these affirmations on cards, post them where you can see them often, and repeat them daily. This practice helps to internalize your worth and the necessity of boundaries, solidifying your commitment to self-care and emotional protection.

Heartfelt Reflections: A Journey Within

Embarking on a journey of self-discovery often involves the critical task of setting and respecting personal boundaries.

Journal Prompt 1: Reflecting on Successful Boundary Setting

Think back to a recent interaction where you successfully set a boundary. Reflect on how you felt before taking that step—were you anxious, determined, or something else? As you went through the process of setting the boundary, notice what emotions surfaced. Afterward, did you feel relief, empowerment, or perhaps uncertainty about your actions? Write about what this experience taught you about your needs and how effectively setting boundaries can serve to protect and honor your inner child.

_____

_____

_____

_____

_____

_____

_____

_____

_____

_____

_____

_____

_____

_____

_____

_____

_____

_____

_____

Journal Prompt 2: Learning from Missed Boundaries

Recall a moment when you failed to set a boundary and later wished you had. What were the circumstances, and what held you back? Consider the emotional aftermath of this incident—how did it affect your mood, self-esteem, or stress levels? Reflect on how this situation impacted your inner child. Moving forward, how might you handle a similar situation differently to better safeguard your emotional well-being?

_____

_____

_____

_____

_____

_____

_____

_____

_____

_____

_____

_____

_____

_____

_____

_____

_____

_____

_____

Journal Prompt 3: Evaluating Self-Imposed Limits

Consider the boundaries you currently have with yourself. Are there limits you should be enforcing to better care for your inner child? Maybe it's setting a bedtime to ensure you get enough rest, or perhaps it's limiting self-criticism and allowing yourself more grace. Describe these boundaries and outline practical steps you plan to take to implement them. How will these self-imposed limits help you nurture a healthier, more compassionate relationship with yourself?

_____

_____

_____

_____

_____

_____

_____

_____

_____

_____

_____

_____

_____

Through these reflections, you can better understand how boundaries affect your emotional land-scape and how strengthening them can significantly enhance your ability to care for your inner child.

CONCLUSION

As we draw this journey to a close, it's important to pause and reflect on the ground we've covered together in this workbook. From the initial steps of recognizing and understanding the needs of your inner child to embracing the processes that foster healing and growth, you've embarked on a profound path toward inner peace.

You now hold a toolkit brimming with strategies and insights—each exercise, reflection, and challenge has been a stepping stone to a deeper understanding of yourself and your emotional landscapes. You've learned the importance of listening to your inner child, recognizing their cries for attention that were perhaps ignored or misunderstood in the past. Through various exercises, you've practiced speaking to yourself with kindness, setting boundaries that protect and honor your needs, and engaging in self-care that nurtures your physical and emotional well-being.

It's important to acknowledge the courage it takes to confront and heal the wounds of your inner child. This work isn't easy. It requires vulnerability, honesty, and a willingness to change long-established patterns of thinking and feeling. But as you've probably begun to notice, the rewards of such courage are immense. Finding peace within yourself, feeling more integrated and whole, can enrich every aspect of your life—from your relationships with others to your sense of purpose and fulfillment.

As you move forward, remember that healing is not a linear process. There will be days when old pains resurface or when your newly established boundaries are tested. In these moments, lean on the tools and techniques you've cultivated. Use your journaling skills to navigate confusing emotions, revisit exercises that brought you insight, and continuously remind yourself of the affirmations that lift your spirits.

In this workbook, you've laid down the foundational work, but the healing journey is ongoing. Each day offers a new opportunity to nurture your inner child and to build upon the peace you've started to establish.

So, as you turn the final page of this workbook, don't view it as the end of your journey but as a commencement. You are now equipped with knowledge, strategies, and a deeper awareness of your needs and strengths. Move forward with the confidence that you have everything you need to continue nurturing and protecting your inner child. Your path toward lasting peace and happiness is ever-evolving, and you are well-prepared to walk it with resilience and grace. Thank you for having the courage to start on this path, and may your journey be rich with discovery and transformation.

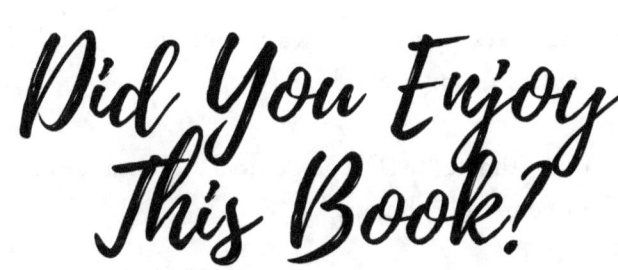

Did You Enjoy This Book?

Thank you for purchasing our book! We're delighted you've chosen to embark on this journey with us. Your support means the world to us, and we sincerely hope you found joy, inspiration, and valuable insights in these pages.

If you enjoyed this book, we would be immensely grateful if you could leave a review or recommend it to others.

Your feedback helps us grow and enables other readers to discover this work.

REFERENCES

❦

Boerger, L. (2023, August 29). 22 ways to connect with your inner child. Made With Lemons. https://madewithlemons.co/connect-with-your-inner-child/

Compitus, K. (2024, March 5). Your ultimate EMDR guide (incl.. Techniques & Exercises). PositivePsychology.com. https://positivepsychology.com/emdr-therapy/

Cooks-Campbell, A. (2024, March 6). How inner child work enables healing and playful discovery. The Most Comprehensive Coaching Platform. https://www.betterup.com/blog/inner-child-work?hs_amp=true#causes

Hopkins Medicine. (2021, November 1). Forgiveness: Your health depends on it. Johns Hopkins Medicine. https://www.hopkinsmedicine.org/health/wellness-and-prevention/forgiveness-your-health-depends-on-it

Hoshaw, C. (2022, March 29). What mindfulness really means and how to practice. Healthline. https://www.healthline.com/health/mind-body/what-is-mindfulness

Kapur, J. (2023, July 3). Childhood trauma: Identifying the origins of inner wounds. Sportskeeda. https://www.sportskeeda.com/health-and-fitness/childhood-trauma-identifying-origins-inner-wounds

Raypol, C. (2020, June 26). Inner child: 6 ways to find yours. Healthline. https://www.healthline.com/health/inner-child

Shiraz, Z. (2022, May 21). Steps to healing childhood trauma as an adult. Hindustan Times. https://www.hindustantimes.com/lifestyle/relationships/steps-to-healing-childhood-trauma-as-an-adult-101653116132187-amp.html

Smith, M. (2024, February 5). EMDR therapy for trauma, PTSD, anxiety, and panic. HelpGuide.org. https://www.helpguide.org/articles/therapy-medication/emdr-therapy.htm

Willey, W. (2020, March 20). Wonderment. Thrive Global. https://community.thriveglobal.com/wonderment/#:~:text=Wonderment%20is%20also%20being%20able,being%20amazed%20by%20simple%20things